FOREIGNER IN CHARGE

FOREIGNER IN CHARGE

Success strategies for
expat leaders in Australia

Padraig O'Sullivan

Foreigner in Charge: Success strategies for expat leaders in Australia
First published 2014

Kerryman Media
56 The Strand
Gladesville NSW 2111, Australia
www.osullivanfield.com
Copyright © 2014 Padraig O'Sullivan
Padraig O'Sullivan asserts the moral right to be identified as the author
of this work.

A CiP catalogue record for this book is available at the
National Library of Australia

ISBN 978-0-9941585-0-5

Edited by Karen Gee
Text typeset by Midland Typesetters, Australia
Cover design by Saso
Printed by Griffin Press

CONTENTS

TESTIMONIALS ABOUT PADRAIG 'POD' O'SULLIVAN

'He is a true thought leader. I always come away from our time together feeling inspired.'
—*Simon Youngs, Global Head of Learning, Coats*

'My coaching sessions with Padraig were critical in helping me see deeper into the challenges I was having and how my reactions affected the people around me.'
—*David Gibbons, COO, BBC Worldwide*

'Having worked with Padraig for two years, he has provided invaluable support and guidance. He offers a different perspective by asking the hard questions and helping reframe each situation to uncover the real opportunity for knowledge, organisational development, learning and self-improvement.'
—*Steve Keys, Senior Vice President, Software AG Asia Pacific and Middle East*

'Padraig is a world-class coach whom any senior executive would benefit from. He was the ideal coach to guide me through a significant professional and cultural transition.'
—*Martin Grossman, Managing Director ANZ, Actelion Pharmaceuticals*

'Padraig was an outstanding executive coach for me, dare I say, was a successful leader but contemplating my own set of key questions and development challenges. We connected easily and focused on the outcomes I was after. He is an incredible listener, highly insightful, honest and experienced in his counsel and coaching. The program was more helpful and defining than I'd imagined.'
—*Pete Everingham, CEO Seek Asia*

'I can't really put my finger on what he said, untapped or triggered to spark such a turnaround in who I am as an executive. However, what I can tell you is that I have been on a good to great journey ever since I met him! Padraig intelligently leads you down a path of self-discovery, which can be confronting but well worth the journey.'
—*Teresa Warren, Melbourne Convention Bureau*

'In moving to NZ to join the leadership team, the content of this book gave me invaluable tools to balance making a positive impact while assimilating to the new environment. Padraig applies his strong emotional intelligence and his vast experience of professional coaching and team building insights to bring you this simple and useful guide. An excellent professional and personal journey, as well as a great read.'
—*Bevan Adin, Managing Director, Beam Global (NZ)*

'Padraig O'Sullivan understands leadership and understands how people can come together to collectively succeed in the work environment. His powerful insights and logical advice have been of immense benefit to me and the teams I've led. Padraig is an incredibly insightful and pragmatic coach, who kept reminding me "Leaders lead" and "There is little risk in practising different leadership styles but plenty of upside".'
—*Alex Condoleon, Medical Director Sanofi, China*

'As the new MD of the Australian affiliate of a global company coming from overseas, Padraig O'Sullivan's coaching sped up by several months the induction into my new job and the onset of my added value to my business and organisation.

'Padraig's thoughtful preparation of our monthly sessions, outstanding questioning and listening skills fast-tracked my learning of the Australian business and people culture in general and of my own affiliate in particular. Through the development of an acute self-awareness of my strengths and weaknesses in the face of these, he was a catalyst to focus my leadership on the right issues and opportunities.'
—*James Priour, Managing Director, Amgen Australia/NZ*

'There has been much written about the failure rates of expats across the world. With this book we now have a well-developed guide on how to actually succeed as an expatriate business leader.'
—*Dr Gordon Spence, Director of Masters Business Coaching program, Sydney Business School*

'I have had the pleasure of working with Padraig O'Sullivan in a number of roles and across a variety of organisations throughout my career. What separates Padraig from others is his ability to truly and quickly get to the essence of people and situations regardless of the complexity, to connect and build trust and coach people to focus on the things that will really make the biggest difference for their leadership and their organisation. This is especially valuable in times of increasing complexity and globalisation where businesses require more from leaders than ever before.'
—*Jill Tapping, Human Resources, Eli Lilly*

'A must-read for any expat appointed to a leadership position in Australia. The book's engaging case studies and analogies, backed by proven and practical frameworks, also form a valuable resource for any newly appointed CEO.'
—*Stephen Shepherd, Founding Partner, Altus Q*

'The advice and guidance that I received allowed me to make some material changes to my routine and focus which had an immediate positive impact (personally and professionally). The work we did together helped me work through some challenging times and ensured that I am better armed to deal with issues in the future.'
—*Jonathan Engle, International Marketing Director, Software of Excellence (A Henry Schein Co.)*

'Padraig has brought his blend of practicality and theory to bear on a crucially economic topic for international businesses. The theory is never left high and dry but is rooted in reality, whether case study or practical wisdom. A workman-like book by an excellent coach.'
—*Robin Linnecar, co-author of* Business Coaching *and Founding Chairperson, Praesta International*

FOREWORD

Being tapped to advance to a job assignment overseas can be a great opportunity — there is risk and potential for great reward. However, being successful in one context is not an indicator that a leader will remain successful in another, particularly if that context is foreign. Pitfalls abound not only in assimilating to a new cultural context but in the ability to acclimatise to the new position, new colleagues and, in many facets, new ways of doing business. Among the hazards facing such executives are their own 'proven' successful behaviours that got them this opportunity in the first place. How could they anticipate that what got them where they are could now be their greatest obstacle to success?

Padraig O'Sullivan has spent years as an executive coach and is a Certified Marshall Goldsmith Stakeholder Centered Coach working with successful executives helping them to become better leaders. Stakeholder Centered Coaching is a method I developed requiring leaders to identify and make changes in their behaviour; it focuses on leaders who want to improve — which is half the battle. The remainder of the process involves bringing about an accurate self-awareness of habits that actually inhibit achievement and alienate colleagues in a cross-cultural environment. Padraig has seen that these kinds of behaviours — if left unacknowledged, unchecked and unchallenged — can result in a staggering failure rate for expatriate executives.

Engaging stakeholders and placing a strong emphasis on action, implementation and follow-through is essential if leaders truly want to succeed. Padraig emphasises this in his coaching work and in this helpful text. Multinational businesses require more from leaders as they must effectively direct geographically dispersed and culturally diverse teams. And it all must be done *now*.

Leadership lessons can be learnt; and one of my favourite methods is through storytelling, which in many cases translates well across cultures. I love the way a good story can communicate a concept to people, so that they can relate and identify with it in a visceral way rather than grapple with understanding jargon. Padraig is an excellent communicator and storyteller whose anecdotes bring practical meatiness to the bones of theory creating a text of substance and value. I commend him for his passion to focus on the often overlooked expatriate executive experience and recommend those who find themselves on the cusp of a business move to Australia to seek out Padraig and to use this book.

Marshall Goldsmith

Marshall's Stakeholder Centered Coaching methodology, which guarantees measurable leadership growth combined with his global network of certified executive coaches, has been the world's leading executive coaching organisation for many years. Furthermore, Marshall has been recognised as the number one leadership thinker in the world and the number seven business thinker in the world at the biannual Thinkers 50 Ceremony sponsored by the *Harvard Business Review*. Dr Goldsmith's PhD is from UCLA's Anderson School of Management, where in 2010 he was recognised as one of 100 distinguished graduates in the school's 75-year history. He teaches executive education at Dartmouth's Tuck School of Business and frequently speaks at other leading business schools around the world. He is one of a select few executive advisors who have been asked to work with more than 120 major CEOs and their management teams. He served on the board of the Peter Drucker Foundation for ten years.

INTRODUCTION

When James came home to tell his wife he had received a promotion and they would all be heading to Australia, he was really excited. This is what they had been working towards for the last five years. Finally, he was being rewarded for his hard work and was being given the opportunity to lead his own business internationally. His wife was excited and also nervous about the changes lying ahead of them. Three months later they arrived in Sydney with their two small daughters. Finding a home was daunting but they fell in love with their apartment in Mosman overlooking beautiful Balmoral Beach. The kids settled into school and the family found a new rhythm.

Fast forward twelve months and James was having a serious conversation with his boss that ultimately led to him being given a clear and pointed message: 'Shape up or you will be shipped out.' What went wrong?

James made mistakes and errors of judgement over those twelve months that negatively impacted his leadership credibility and lay the path for his eventual demise in the role and exit out of the organisation. So how could someone of his capability and experience end up making these mistakes? How did the organisation, a well-respected multinational company in the health care sector with hundreds of international assignments on the go, fail to set him up for success? Why did the local leadership team let this happen? Was he sabotaged? What could he have done differently to create a different outcome?

Unfortunately this is not a made up story. It is real, and it illustrates an all too common outcome for expatriate leaders. Studies put the failure rate at between 25 and 50 per cent.[1] Internal hires, in general, fail at a rate of approximately 20 to 30 per cent and this rises up to 50 per cent when international expatriate assignments are included. Failure most often occurs at or before the eighteen-month mark.

When you consider the obvious cost of a) recruitment, b) international relocation, c) transport, d) housing and accommodation, e) school fees and other benefits associated with expatriate assignments, the cost of expatriate leaders is enormous. In general, the cost is deemed to be between two to three times the total package. This does not account for the hidden expenses including the time and focus of the organisational resources at both home and host locations. So when the assignment fails this is a significant expense for the organisation. It has been suggested that for senior executives whose base salary is above US$250,000, the cost of a failed expatriate assignment can be up to 40 times base salary.[2] So what is failure?

A failed expatriate assignment, at a professional and developmental level, is defined under three categories:

• the assignment is ceased early and the executive is recalled home;
• the executive is returned to their original position upon the end of the assignment; or
• the executive is deemed to have not performed adequately and leaves the organisation.

For some industries, such as the mining industry, many expatriate roles are set up on a project basis with full expectation that the leader will return to their original role. This is not defined as failure, of course.

On a personal level, it has been reported that almost 50 per cent of expatriate marriages end in divorce, accelerated by the stress caused by international assignments.[3]

But there is hope

This book emerged from The Expat Program, a professional service delivered through the consulting business I founded, OSullivanField. Our work with expatriate leaders has developed in response to organisational requests to support leaders arriving in Australia. This holistic program has been developed to meet the needs of the expatriate leader, their family and the employing organisation.

We noticed there seemed to be seven foundation principles:

1. All executives arriving in Australia want to be successful, and their families have made sacrifices to allow and support that success. No one embarks on an international assignment planning to fail. No one

makes the effort to travel across the world to live in a foreign country while harbouring the notion that this might derail their career rather than be a building block.

2. Coming to Australia can be viewed (by the expatriate and/or their family) as being anywhere from a major inconvenience to a grand adventure. Generally, Australia is seen to be an exciting, desirable location, familiar enough so as not to be thought of as harbouring great difficulties.

   However, our clients tell us they are often surprised at the challenges they encounter. Expatriate communities are not as visible as they are in countries such as Singapore or Japan, so connecting with people in similar situations is not always easy. There is a lack of support that might be available in other countries, for example in the areas of domestic help and childcare. While Australians are deemed to be very friendly this is often seen to be at a superficial level, so social connectivity does not come easily. Expatriates talk about their need to work very hard to build up relationships while in Australia. Their enjoyment of the country and lifestyle remains with them long after they leave but it is often seen to be an adventure that is less exciting than they expected.

3. There are core transitions every expatriate goes through when taking on a new assignment. Successful expatriate leaders manage these core transitions, learn the new culture at personal, family, team, organisational and country levels while delivering to assignment requirements.

4. While every leader is unique in their own right, we have never experienced a 100 per cent unique assignment! All leaders who embark on an expatriate assignment experience the same core transitions and often encounter similar issues at leadership levels in their new affiliate. While the mandate they have been given as a leader in the new affiliate may vary from one organisation to the next, the pathways towards success are well known, well trodden and easily understood.

5. Successful expatriate leaders work hard at building credibility and minimising damage that may occur through mistakes they inevitably and inadvertently make. They understand credibility is needed to gain the buy-in of peers, colleagues and direct reports to execute their mandate. This credibility is earned — it is not a right.

6. Given the natural ambition of expatriate leaders, the need to develop core transferable skills is essential. There are nine core skills every expatriate leader needs to master and these will apply to every role upon which the leader embarks. These are outlined at the start of 'Part 2: PALDER — A framework for expatriate leadership' and at the beginning of each chapter in this section.

7. Given the cost of each assignment and the cost of failure it is important that you, your family and the organisation all win by having a
   successful expatriate assignment. Implementing an integrated support
   program for an expatriate leader can increase the likelihood of success
   by two- to threefold.

Why this book now?

A 2011 HSBC study suggests that Australia is the second most desirable
expatriate destination in the world. Over 70 per cent of respondents said
they planned and were seeking an expatriate assignment in Australia. Next
to the United Kingdom and Canada, Australia is seen as a very worthwhile
and 'safe' destination for new expatriates. The maturity of the overall
business market, the safety of our political system, the sophistication of
our education system and the proximity to Asia are all seen as reasons to
support Australia as an expatriate destination for multinational companies.
Despite having a global market share of between 1 and 3 per cent, Australia
regularly contributes the majority of revenue at an Asia regional level and
therefore expatriate leaders working in Australia also get to see business
from an Asia perspective while at their Sydney or Melbourne offices.

As outlined earlier, the failure rates for expatriate leaders are quite stark.
The fact that expatriate leaders experience multiple transitions at the same
time, and often for the first time, increases the likelihood of failure.

Yet there has been and will always be many successful expatriate leaders
who have led organisations within Australia. These leaders leave a clear
pathway to achieving their view of what success looks like. They have had
the ability to develop interpersonal skills that relate at a local level. They
have learnt to listen and learn and look for cultural norms that are different to what they have experienced before and to use these cultural norms
as accelerators, as opposed to inhibitors, of change. Successful expatriate
leaders have understood the need to manage their own transition and that
of their family while executing the task for which they were employed.
Finally, successful expatriate leaders are able to align their personal goals
with those of the organisation both locally and internationally, and are
able to consciously forge a path that will satisfy the needs of all parties.

Psychologists suggest that a pre-assessment of core traits can lead to
predictive success rates. The ability to be open, vulnerable, keen to learn
and the desire to enjoy the new and local culture are traits deemed to
help executives be successful in a new environment. But our experience
suggests this is not enough. Having worked with hundreds of expatriate

executives in Australia we also understand that transitioning into the country, from a cultural perspective, is only part of the overall success. Being able to successfully transition to a new level of leadership in a remote, unfamiliar and unsupported environment is also a key part of the executive success. Lastly, being able to lead and guide one's family to fully enjoy the experience in Australia and leave with lasting positive memories is a critical element to ensure a successful expatriate assignment.

Different approaches

Organisations that support expatriates tend to fall into four different categories with regards to the support they offer expats and their families.

Little or no support
The organisation provides very basic relocation, transport, accommodation assistance and basic information about office logistics. This satisfies the basic, short-term transactional needs and rarely goes beyond the first week after arrival in the country.

Cultural support
Many organisations offer short programs on explaining the cultural differences between Australia and their host country, and the family of the executive are often included. Some organisations give insight into Australian history, the political system and the education system. While most executives are grateful for the information, many comment that it is while learning to lead the organisation over the ensuing three, six and twelve months that they really start to understand the Australian culture.

Financial and logistics support
Many organisations are generous in assisting expatriate relocation through financial and insurance means. While very welcome and financially rewarding, they do not necessarily assist the expatriate leader to settle into the new role itself.

Role support
Executive coaching is a well-utilised and known mechanism for supporting executives to transition into the role. Learning to elevate the level of thinking that needs to be employed, the level of leadership required for the new position and the level of influence needed across the organisation is as much a nurtured and learnt framework as it is a natural ability. Many

organisations support executives by providing an internal or external coach to work alongside them for the first three to six months. Traditionally an executive coach will focus on the role only and will not take into account the multiple transitions the executive is experiencing.

A more integrated approach

Our experience at OSullivanField is that for expatriate leaders to maximise their effectiveness and for organisations to attempt to ensure success, an integrated program of support needs to be offered. This book is based upon such a program.

An integrated support program ensures all five transitions are managed and the executive is planning for and executing each phase of the transition from the day they arrive to the end of the first year. The skills needed for each phase are explored and are, if need be, developed in conjunction with their coach. Preparation and practice for the highly visible events where the leader is on show are conducted e.g. messaging on the first day, first leadership team meeting, first town hall (whole of company) presentation to the wider organisation, the strategy development and cascading down the organisation and many other public events where the credibility of the leader is being tested by their audience.

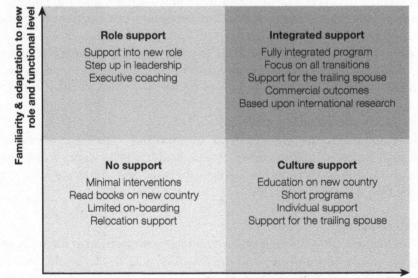

Figure 1: Levels of support

Understanding the natural human fear that sits with every leader around potential failure, an integrated program helps build resilience and self-confidence by using evidence-based strategies from positive psychology.

Learning to lead remotely while managing up in a different part of the world is a skill most expatriate leaders have not yet mastered when they arrive in Australia. The need to do so is essential given the organisation has expectations of successful transitions that are probably more demanding than the reality of how fast executives can transition on an expatriate assignment.

Helping the family to prepare and integrate into a new country by introducing them to strategies and circles of friends and acquaintances decreases the potential risk for instability and allows for a more successful family experience.

Our hope for this book

This book emerged from our work. It captures the conversations and the pathways developed for expatriate leaders to follow to ensure their success in Australia. It shares suggestions to enable you to explore new ways of leading and to lead successfully internationally.

My hope for the book lies in four key areas.

Your success
Given the risk and the ambition that lies in every expatriate assignment we hope you will have a successful assignment. You bring with you international experience that is valuable to the organisation. You leave with experience that will shape and fashion your leadership for the next and future assignments.

The local team benefits
We hope the Australian team will be enhanced. Australian teams and individuals can learn from their international colleagues who arrive here on assignment and indeed develop their own international career path in a similar way. As globalisation continues, the need to have wider and varying perspectives than those gained in your own country will become essential. Having worked for expatriate leaders, Australian-based executives will naturally widen their own perspective. For the leaders involved in recruiting the new expatriate to Australia, we hope the decision proves worthy.

The organisation benefits

We hope Australian organisations continue to embrace expatriate leaders and provide them with every opportunity to be successful. The advantage Australia has is its distance from the rest of the world — its distance from global head offices fosters resourcefulness and innovation. The disadvantage Australia has, ironically, is also its distance from the rest of the world. The lack of any shared geographical boundaries with other countries means that we run the risk of being isolated. One of the advantages of expatriate assignments is that organisations as a whole get to increase connectivity to the wider world and become more successful as a result. It is important that Australia continues to develop its reputation as a development ground for executives both inbound and outbound and we believe this book will be useful for both the expatriate leader and those leaders who support expatriate leaders in organisations.

Your family has an adventure

We hope your family will have an adventure to remember and will enjoy their experience in Australia. It is a beautiful country with many spectacular wonders. We hope that, with some careful planning, spontaneity and a dash of courage, expatriate families will reach out and enjoy their time here.

How to use this book

This book is divided into three parts. Part 1: 'Getting your bearings' offers a brief introduction to Australia including history, geography, political and school systems, the sporting environment and a general look at what makes Australia tick. The role of family in an expatriate transition is also discussed in detail — the experience your family has will play a huge part in determining your success in your expatriate assignment. We cover the main points you need to be aware of in relation to your family, along with some thoughts and tips as to how to ensure their experience is a successful one. This section also explores some the unique challenges faced by expat leaders.

Part 2 of the book focuses on you, the expatriate in your role of leader within a business context. We set out a framework, called PALDER, which looks at different phases of transition and explores what stage you should be at on a monthly basis. The core skills of successful expatriate transitions are fully detailed and the outputs associated with each phase explained. Some frameworks are offered that will allow you to assess your leadership team and organisational culture; a framework is also included that is aimed at building team performance and holding the organisation accountable to their leadership mandate. We suggest you read Part 2 and come back to it throughout the next twelve months as you experience each transition in real time.

The final section, Part 3, is designed as a support section to complement the first two. Thoughts are offered on key support networks, how to work, how to work with your leadership team, mentors, confidants and other key figures in your network. Checklists for each stage are available for download, and tip sheets to ensure your success at key events are also available (see www.foreignerincharge.com). A range of online videos are available that illustrate other expatriates' experiences, typical scenarios faced and suggested pathways to success. There is a 'Resources' section at the back of this book that includes a list of useful websites for expats and their families — see page 167.

As with all transitions, your level of openness to change, your ability to learn new things and the degree of vulnerability you are prepared to experience while in transition will determine your overall success. The organisation has invested in bringing you and your family to Australia because it believes you are the best leader for this job right now. This book can help you make that success a reality.

Being an expat in Australia: Padraig's story

Growing up in Ireland I think I always knew I would live abroad. The Irish have moved overseas throughout the ages, sometimes not of their own choosing. Whether due to political or famine reasons we left our home country in our thousands and aimed for all continents. England initially settled many Irish emigrants. Then America called and opened her arms. Over time almost every country in the world had the Irish settle within.

Australia became a natural migration destination. Under British rule many Irish convicts were sent to settle the new country, and over time the Irish kept coming. The weather certainly helped. Anecdotally, today almost one in four Australians can trace roots back to Ireland somehow.

I remember *the* moment really well. Mike Murphy on the RTE television station in Dublin did a six-part TV show, called *Murphy's Australia* in the late 1970s. He traced a range of Irish immigrants to Australia, showcasing their journeys and how Australia had treated them since their arrival. As an eight year old I was amazed at how much Australia seemed to offer. It was referred to as the lucky country and the young child in me totally believed that to be true. Sun, sand, surfing, sailing … while out the window of my bedroom in Ireland I could see sleet, snow and not much else in the pre-Celtic Tiger era! At that point I decided I would eventually live in Australia; however it took almost two decades to actually achieve that, with time living in London and travelling across South East Asia en route.

Actualising the dream has had its ups and downs of course. The sun, sand and surf are exactly as I was led to believe. While I will never be a regular surfer there is no better way to spend a Friday evening after work between October and March than having an outdoor barbecue with friends after a dip in the water at a Sydney beach. I remember my first couple of weeks after arriving in Adelaide — I woke up most mornings to hear laughing. It took me a while to realise I was waking to the sound of kookaburras singing, which I found really humorous. Over the years I am still amazed at the animal life, the bushwalks, the native fauna that is Australia. While I have seen many parts of the country, I still have lots to explore.

The humidity and heat of Adelaide and then Sydney took some time to get used to. Even today, almost twenty years later, I underestimate the power of the sun to burn one's skin.

Australia is a society that travels a lot. Everyone goes overseas regularly be it to Bali, London or the United States. What surprised me is that university students don't travel. There seems to be a natural 'leaving the home nest' in many countries when children leave home to go to university. Maybe Australians are saving for their overseas trips but university students seem to live at home for a good many years. I have regularly reminded my children of their European heritage when it came to planning university choices, i.e. feel free to leave home!

Settling in I had to learn about a crucial part of Australian life. Whether or not I admired Don Bradman*, even if I didn't know who he was, it did not matter — in this country there is no other choice but to learn about sports. The best conversations start when two people argue the various merits of their preferred sporting codes and teams. Eventually I settled on rugby league, otherwise my conversations with the in-laws would have been doomed to brevity.

For me, Christmas will always be a time of snow, cold weather, hats, scarves and hot toddies. A barbecue on the beach wearing T-shirts and thongs does not quite do it for me. It never will.

The casual nature of work deceived me over time. Initially Australians can appear to not really care about work. However, the reality is Australians work hard, efficiently and will do what it takes to get their work done so they can leave to enjoy 'life'. I still notice that many Australians come to work really early and leave early, relative to other countries. I have regularly seen people (not in leadership roles) at their desks at 7 a.m. The daylight and bright sun facilitates this. While many people in Australia are identified by their work, the country as a society is not. The problem for many expat leaders is the perception that has been built up that Australians are lazy/not committed/unwilling to go the extra mile when they are not present for a 7–9 p.m. tele-conference call on a Friday night. Meanwhile, the Australian is happily enjoying life and will return to work on Monday recharged and ready to go.

Coffee meetings are important. In Europe, when a prospective client agrees to have a coffee meeting they are doing just that: having coffee. It is not a sign that they are ready to do business, as it is in Australia. This took me a while to learn and more than a few disappointments to get over.

As someone who has always made their own way in life I naturally gravitated to the Australian sense of independence. 'Punching above your weight' is natural for Australians. I suspect the distance and time zones from everywhere else (i.e. head offices in the United States, United Kingdom or Europe) make this possible. Why? I think the distance, or more specifically the time zones, allows for less interference or micro-managing from abroad; there are fewer opportunities for senior leaders to travel to local offices. This also leads to an increased need to be innovative and resourceful at a local level, as the lack of regular contact means Australians are left to their own devices. I found this quite easy to adapt to given my age when I arrived in Australia but also because of its similarities to Ireland. But I have noticed many expat leaders from the United States, parts of Europe and other countries where responding to hierarchy is valued, do not appreciate this societal trait.

Finally, I got used to having my name shortened. Everyone's name gets shortened eventually. Even if your original name has one syllable the locals will shorten it. Today, this is how I introduce myself to strangers: 'My name's Padraig, but all my friends calls me Pod; feel free to do so.' It's easier. It's the Australian way. The lucky country.

*Most famous Australian cricketer ever and all-round legend.

PART 1

GETTING YOUR BEARINGS

1

TRANSITION OVERLOAD

As the expectations of leaders and of leadership have increased in recent times so too has our tolerance for poor leadership decreased. The average tenure for a publicly listed CEO is now less than three years.[1] When we consider the demands we put upon our leaders it is no wonder the failure rates can be very high.

With expatriate leaders, however, there are nuances to the causes of failure that are unique to the assignment. Primarily, multiple transitions are experienced simultaneously, compounded with this often being the first time this has occurred in the expatriate's career.

Compound issues

Compare the experience of an executive living in Paris who is, say, managing a marketing function. They are then promoted to group head of marketing. In this scenario, the only real transition is their level of responsibility and peer group. There are no changes for them at an organisation familiarity level, at a family level, at a functional expertise level or indeed a cultural level. However, if the same head of marketing is then promoted to take on the general manager role of the Australian affiliate, they will experience multiple transitions simultaneously and often for the first time.

Increased responsibility

Their role increases in responsibility from a functional role to a general role. They are now required to sync across multiple functions. Their previous functional expertise, while useful and having served them well to the point of being promoted to this role, could hinder their success if overreliance in this area hinders an ability to adopt a general management approach. They need to elevate and expand their thinking and perspective in a horizontal fashion as opposed to the old vertical fashion.

Increased complexity

The level of complexity dramatically increases as often does the number of direct reports. Using our Paris example, this person would typically move from having a function of twenty to 30 reports in Paris to responsibility for 300 to 500 reports in Australia. Clearly, the opposite can also happen if someone was, for example, a Sales Director in the United States and is now the Australian Managing Director. They may experience a decrease in overall numbers from, say, 2000 sales representatives to 400 or 500 reports in Australia.

Whichever way it works, the implication is that how things worked in the old scenario are not necessarily going to be appropriate or effective in the new.

Increased visibility

Becoming the country head brings a level of visibility to external stakeholders that expatriate leaders have often never experienced before. Depending on their sector and industry speciality they may now be asked to represent the organisation at political meetings, with statutory regulatory authorities and other external stakeholders. This requires a unique approach and skill set.

Cultural transition

The cultural transition from one country to another can be daunting. Expatriate leaders are often surprised at the impact the cultural transition to Australia has upon them. Some clients suggest their experience of moving to an Asian-speaking country is easier as they at least expected cultural differences.

The assumed level of familiarity with Australia for leaders from English-speaking countries deceives them. They expect it to be easy but it is not. For leaders who come from non-English speaking countries, learning to lead in English can add an extra dimension of complexity.

Increased pressure on self

Given the ambitious nature of expatriate leaders, they can easily adopt a 'do whatever it takes' mentality in order to be successful in their new role. While this is easily understood and laudable, it can also become a derailer when the checks and balances they had access to in their previous roles might not be available to them. For example, when someone has worked at head office they are used to having support networks within easy access and often down the same corridor. The ability to pop into your leader's office for a quick five-minute chat, an end-of-day review or a pre-meeting advice session is easily underestimated.

They undertake their new role in the presence of remote leadership, often for the first time. When the same leader moves to a different part of the world where they are now remote from the support network, operating in different time zones, they could find they have to schedule meetings with their leader. This is compounded by the fact that they have also inherited a new boss with whom there might be no pre-existing relationship.

The combination of these factors can lead the expatriate to develop and execute unchecked leadership behaviours and patterns that are not helpful to the achievement of success in the role or for the organisation.

Family stresses

All of these transitions so far are happening at the individual executive level. For the expatriate leader their families are also undergoing a major transition, often for the very first time. The families have left their homes, known environments, schools and friends and landed in Australia. Most arrive looking forward to the experience and fully intend to make the most of their overseas assignment. Yet studies suggests that between 21 to 57 per cent of families fail to adapt on international assignments, which greatly impacts the executive.

Quite often the executive already knows people within the international organisation who are living in Australia and therefore has a degree of familiarity with people before they arrive. Given they are also busy at work and determined to succeed, they are occupied for many hours of the week. The family, especially the trailing spouse, are often left to their own devices to make their way in a new and strange environment. This can create stress and tension, which is neither fun for anyone nor conducive to good work performance.

When you combine all of these transitions and know they are happening all at once and, for most expat executives, for the first time, it is easy to understand why the failure rates can be so high. It used to be that expatriates who went on assignment landed in one country and stayed there for many years, thus enabling them to build up long-term friendships at a local level. However, the typical assignment for an expatriate family is now just under three years and most expatriates will have a minimum of three assignments before they are repatriated. The ability to be able to overcome the challenge of these transitions is essential for the executive, their family and the organisation.

How long does it take to come up to speed?

In his book *The First 90 Days*, Michael Watkins suggests every leader needs to be up to speed within 90 days. This concept is well accepted. Lee Hecht Harrison suggest in their 2012 'Insights report' that within 90 days a leader can win friends and influence people. Steve Sargent, the Australian GE leader, suggests that within 90 days of starting, a new leader learns what needs to be done, has mapped out a plan to achieve this and has made the decisions as to what will be done.[2]

It is unreasonable to expect a leader to have fully transitioned into a new role, particularly an expatriate role, within 90 days. Given the number of transitions at play, our experience is that most expatriate leaders take between four and ten months to transition into their roles.

Given the popularity of 90-day plans, though, organisations are looking for evidence of successful transitions earlier than executives are sometimes able to do. While officially evaluations of performance take place after the twelve-month mark of an expat transition into a new role, unofficially the evaluations start after the three-month mark and before six months. Therefore, if there is a suspicion or concern of underperformance the organisation is 'watching for evidence' from the six-month mark onwards. A series of cultural, leadership and personal interventions have to happen from the commencement of the expat assignment in order to give a positive indication to the organisation that progress is being made (see Figure 2).

Research from the Institute for Executive Development suggests that 62 per cent of executives believed it took them more than six months to transition into the role and come up to speed. Even with that, 34 per cent of the same executives had left the role within two years for reasons related to poor performance.

The same research study suggests that almost 50 per cent of organisations use an internal mentoring program to help internal executives transition to new roles. They report this is effective in less than 30 per cent of cases. The report suggests that coaching is a more preferable activity to mentoring as coaching focuses on specific skills and behaviours that need to be honed quickly and adapted to the local cultural environment. The Wynhurst Group, a talent management organisation in the United States, suggests that a structured program is 58 per cent more likely to enable success for transitioning executives. Irrespective of all the research, there is no doubt that for expatriate leaders embarking on international assignments, particularly their first one, the break-even point for speed to competency is longer than a transition that occurs in their own city or within their own company at head office.

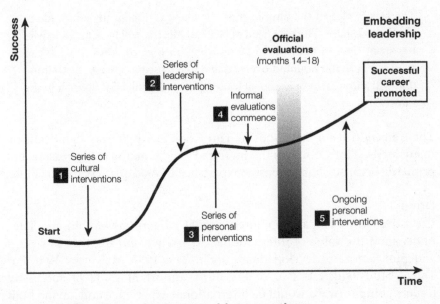

Figure 2: Timeline of integrated interventions

Trends in expatriate assignments within Australia

The CEO Forum Group released the report 'The Expatriate Experience in Australia' in November 2012. Within that they suggest the long-term trend is that expatriate assignments have increased and will continue to increase in the future. This trend has been driven by two key factors.

Broader experience required

Global companies increasingly need leaders with broad international experience. As the global financial crisis hit the western world in the last decade, emerging markets in Asia, South America and other regions have become more important.

Leaders with experience in non-familiar markets have become even more important. Jeff Immelt, the current GE CEO, commented during a recent visit to Australia on the increased diversity of international leaders within his organisation. He explained that for the organisation to continue to grow it needed to develop leadership from emerging markets such as Asia and South America. Indeed, this is a follow-on from Jack Welch, who upon his retirement suggested:

The Jack Welch of the future cannot be like me. I spent my entire life in the United States. The next head of General Electric will be somebody who has spent time in Bombay, in Hong Kong, in Buenos Aires. We have to send our best and brightest overseas and make sure they have the training that will allow them to be global leaders who will make GE flourish in the future.[3]

The transition from Steve Jobs to Tim Cook at Apple was significant on many levels. Tim Cook was the preferred candidate for many reasons but primarily because of his extensive experience in Asia, particularly in China.

Drive

Executives who embark on international careers are ambitious. They understand the value of international experience and use that as a push and pull factor to develop their career. The 1998 McKinsey War For Talent Study suggests two of the most important traits of successful leaders going forward would be international experience and having built the capability to manage and overcome transitions at various times of their career. The CEO Forum Study noted that while the cost of using expatriate managers has increased, including the changes in the living away from home allowances (LAFHA), this will, over time, have a neutral impact on the usage of expatriate leaders.

The motivation for an expat assignment theoretically arises because there is no one available at a local level with the skills and competencies to perform the role so the organisation needs to source someone internationally. However, the use of expatriate assignments is more complex.

Multinational organisations will use countries like Australia as a developmental ground for executives deemed to be on a high potential pathway. Also, when entering new markets such as Australia, organisations often consider they need specialised experience and if they cannot find someone appropriate locally they will look within their own ranks internationally.

Historically, expats came from the parent company or head office. However, as expatriate assignments continue to evolve, it is now more common for expatriates to be third-country nationals (TCNs), i.e. they come from a country different to both that of the head office location and the country where they are working. In an Australian context, companies with head offices in places such as the United States or the United Kingdom are using leaders from Asia, the Middle East and Eastern Europe to gain experience in Australia. While this is a very welcome and natural evolution it raises the challenges associated with cultural transitions when the third country national is coming from a country that is not as familiar with western-based cultures.

China's increasing importance

The range of destinations for expatriates is increasing. Given the increasing prominence of China in global economic terms, having assignments either in or close to China is considered to be important. If this is not possible, having assignments in countries that regularly trade with or are situationally close to China becomes a second-best choice. A mobility study from Ernst and Young in 2011 suggested that 60 per cent of multinational companies had increased their expat assignments in emerging markets in the previous three years and expected to further increase this in the following three years. Therefore expatriate assignments to Australia will continue to be considered important.

Gender differences

There is a gender distinction happening with expatriate assignments. While men still make up the majority, the number of female expatriates is increasing. The CEO Forum Study quotes Relocate, a UK organisation, who suggest the percentage of female expatriates has risen from 3 per cent in the early 1980s to 17 per cent in 2010.[4] From a gender diversity perspective this is a good thing! It does heighten social and family issues purely because the family mother is also the business leader and therefore not the person who is predominantly at home.

Many expatriate female leaders who have children talk privately about the struggle between their career choices and parenting choices. From a practical perspective they often feel it is more difficult to make friends outside of work as they are less involved in school activities.

Other changes

There is a distinct trend with multinationals to decrease the overall lucrative packages that were at one time associated with being an expatriate. Many organisations are moving from expatriate remuneration to localised or localised plus packages, where remuneration is held at a similar level to that of a local hired executive in the same position.

For the families involved in undertaking the assignment, the level of attraction has decreased. However the long-term benefits of having international experience has probably increased and therefore overall sits at a neutral cost. Finally, the kind of assignments and length of assignments has also changed. There is an increase in shorter term assignments of two to three years and a definite increase in project-based assignments where an executive will go to a country for between six and twelve months. For executives with specialised skills or specific project-related skills, the increase in project-based assignments is deemed to be very attractive.

2

WELCOME TO AUSTRALIA

This chapter provides an introduction to Australia's geography and history, its government, its people and culture. It is not intended to be a full resource about Australia, but rather to cover the essential points.

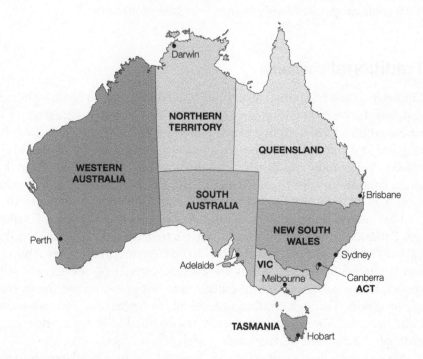

Figure 3: Map of Australia

Geography

Australia is one of the most ancient places on Earth. Originally part of the supercontinent known as Gondwana (which also included Africa, South America, India, Madagascar and New Zealand), Australia split from this larger land mass to become the world's largest island around 50 million years ago. Dinosaur footprints and evidence of coral reefs from an ancient, landlocked sea add to the picture of an age-old land.

Australia is the sixth largest country on the planet. It measures 3700 kilometres from north to south and 4000 kilometres from east to west, and boasts around 8000 kilometres of coastline. By way of comparison, Australia's land mass is almost as large as the United States, and approximately 32 times greater than the United Kingdom. It covers an area of nearly 7.7 million square kilometres, of which approximately 20 per cent is desert. Australia is the lowest and flattest of all the continents, with Mount Kosciuszko being the highest point at only 2228 metres above sea level. However, while it isn't a very high country it does have a wide variety of climatic zones ranging from tropical rainforests to deserts, from cool, temperate forests to snow-covered mountains.

Traditional owners

The original and traditional owners of the land of Australia are the Aboriginal and Torres Strait Islanders, known as Indigenous Australians. It is estimated they have lived in Australia for over 40,000 years. Their lifestyle, religious and cultural traditions reflect a deep connection with the land — indeed, Indigenous Australians' culture is widely accepted as likely the oldest continuous culture on Earth. In 2010 one of the world's oldest stone tools, a 35,000-year-old axe, was found in one of Australia's many deserts.

The indigenous population is estimated to have been between 300,000 and 750,000 at the time European settlers first came to Australia in the 1770s. The first settlers regarded the 500 different and complex Aboriginal languages as babble and as a consequence only 30 dialects are still spoken today. Such an ancient culture was not prepared for the arrival of Europeans. Through conflict, illness and the impacts of negative social influences, the Aboriginal population has declined to today representing just over 2.2 per cent of Australia's population.

Note that at many gatherings in Australia, from official government ceremonies to small school assemblies, it is common for the proceedings to be opened with an acknowledgement of the traditional owners of the land.

Modern 'discovery' and settlement

Australia was sighted and mapped by several different exploring countries before the 1770s. Marco Polo speculated about Australia and maps from the Greeks, Arabs and the Portuguese show outlines of the eastern half of Australia. The Dutchman, Willem Janszoon made Australia's first known landing in 1606 and Abel Tasman followed in 1642 with the sighting of the west coast of Tasmania which he called Van Diemen's Land or New Holland. The voyager William Dampier was looking for new trade routes to the Pacific and was the first Englishman to set foot on the continent in 1688.

The most famous and well documented is Englishman Captain James Cook, who anchored in Botany Bay for a week on 28 April 1770. With the finding of this new continent and the overcrowding in their jails, the British decided they would use Australia as a place to send the unwanted dregs of society: drunks, thieves and criminals. On 26 January 1788 a fleet of eleven ships (now known as the First Fleet) carrying 1000 passengers, three quarters of them convicts, arrived at Port Jackson, just south of Circular Quay in Sydney. Over the following years the British continued to send convicts but also started giving away land in an attempt to settle people away from England. By 1869 the transportation of convicts had stopped and the settlers started to greatly outnumber the convict population, with settlement spreading throughout the country.

The discovery of gold in Bathurst, New South Wales, by Edward Hargraves in May 1851 really put Australia on the map. Prospectors from all over the world rushed to the area. This was the first of many gold finds that attracted a flood of migrants to Australia. By 1880 Australia's population was 2 million and had increased to 6 million by the end of World War I. A further influx of immigrants between 1945 and 1965 increased the population to around 11 million and dramatically changed the cultural, culinary and psychological face of Australia. People from 200 different countries have come to live in Australia and about a quarter of the people currently living here were born overseas. There are more than 200 languages being spoken in Australia with English the official national language.

Government

The Commonwealth of Australia is a constitutional monarchy, a federation and a parliamentary democracy. The Commonwealth of Australia was formed in 1901 as a result of an agreement between six democratic, previously self-governing British colonies. Like the United States, Australia has a written Constitution that defines foreign relations, trade, defence and immigration.

As a constitutional monarchy, the Governor-General is nominated by the Federal Government to represent the Queen as the Head of State. The British Crown in each state is represented by a Governor, now largely a symbolic role.

The Australian federal government, the six states and the two self-governing territories all share the responsibility of governing. There are three levels of government in Australia. The first and the highest of these is the federal government. The federal or commonwealth government is based on a popularly elected parliament headed by the Prime Minister. The second level of government is at state and territory level. These governments adhere to the National Constitution and are responsible for education, transport, health and law enforcement. A Premier who's elected by the political party holding power generally leads them. The third level of government, local government, receives funding from the higher government and rates from local residents. Local governments are responsible for things including town planning, building codes, local roads, water services and community facilities.

The Australian legal system

Australia is a relatively tolerant society where people of many different cultures and backgrounds live together. Migrants to Australia are encouraged to retain and share their traditions and cultures while observing the laws, cultures and customs of Australia.

There are a few areas that are important to highlight.

Equality. In Australia everyone has the right to be treated the same as anyone else, regardless of race or country of origin, sex, marital status, pregnancy, political or religious belief. This applies to employment, accommodation, and purchase of goods and the use of all sorts of services. Men and women are equal by law.

Smoking is generally prohibited in workplaces and most states have also prohibited smoking in restaurants and shopping centres. Signs will indicate where smoking is prohibited but the selling or supplying of cigarettes or tobacco to anyone less than eighteen years of age is prohibited. Drinking and possessing alcohol in some public places is prohibited, as is the supply or sale of alcohol to someone less than eighteen years of age.

Driving laws, particularly in relation to driving after drinking and speeding, are very strict and can result in fines, imprisonment or the loss of licence. The permitted level of blood alcohol may vary throughout Australia. Everyone in a vehicle must use their seatbelt and children require an approved restraint up to the age of seven.

Freedoms

Protected by law, five fundamental freedoms are enjoyed by Australians: the freedoms of speech, association, assembly, religion and movement.

Freedom of speech. Australians are free within the bounds of the law to say or write whatever they think, privately or publicly, about the government or any topic. Free speech, however, should be based on fact rather than rumour.

Freedom of association. Australians are free to join any organisation or group if it's legal. They can choose to belong to a trade union or political party if they wish.

Freedom of assembly. Australians are free to gather in public or in private places for legal, social or political purposes.

Freedom of religion. Australia does not have an official or state religion. The law does not enforce any religious doctrine; however religious practices must conform to the law. You are free to follow any religion you choose, or none at all.

Freedom of movement. In Australia you can move freely to and from all states and territories, and you can leave and return to Australia at any time. Some migrants may have conditions placed on their visa until they become Australian citizens.

The people of Australia

Australia's estimated population is currently over 23 million. The median age in Australia is nearly 40 years, which is nearly five years higher than a decade ago. This shows there is an ageing population and the number of people aged 65 years and over is expected to nearly double in the next 30 years. This is predicted to put significant pressure on resources. Even though it is geographically a massive country, Australia is one of the most urbanised countries in the world. Around 91 per cent of the country's population live in urban areas and 68 per cent live in the southern and eastern states, although there is slow evidence of a trend towards the north and over to Western Australia.

Education

Australia enjoys a wide reputation for academic excellence and offers internationally recognised qualifications. It has one of the highest ratios of enrolment in primary and secondary education in the world. It is a legal requirement that all children attend an approved education institution.

The formal education structure in Australia follows a three-tier model. There are also structures for children before formal education commences. It includes primary education (at primary school) for children aged five to twelve years, followed by secondary education at high school for ages twelve to around eighteen years, and tertiary education (e.g. universities, vocational education and training establishments).

Schools can be classified according to the sources of their funding and their administrative structures. There are three categories in Australia:

- government schools, which are known as public schools or state schools; these are secular although they may offer religious education
- religious-based schools (e.g. Catholic, Anglican)
- independent schools, known as private schools. Some of these are based on cultural backgrounds, such as particular language schools (e.g. an Italian school or a German school).

Around 65 per cent of children in Australia attend public schools and 34 per cent attend private or Catholic schools. The Australian school year runs from January to December with four school terms. The largest holiday is over the Christmas period, during the Australian summer. There are three other two-week school holidays during the year, usually around Easter, July and October.

The cost of attendance at schools can vary widely depending on the type of school and the school itself. International students are required to pay significant additional fees to attend schools in Australia. There are a range of websites that might be useful, listed in the 'Resources' section on page 167.

The Australian lifestyle

Lifestyle is what Australia is really all about. Most Australians live near the coast and regard leisure as a crucial part of their life.

Australia is a sporting nation and most Australians enjoy sport in some form, whether individually or in a team. Not only do they play sport, they watch sport, bet on sport and talk about sport probably more than anything else. It's a very popular topic of conversation; it's also a great socialising and engagement tool.

The Australian climate, landscape and adequate leisure time all provide a wonderful frame for sport to be pursued and enjoyed. There is a massive variety of sports easily available across the entire year and the large number of sporting clubs and teams cover everything from national professional leagues to community-based programs, business and social teams and clubs.

Popular sports include what Australians call soccer, rugby union, rugby league, Aussie rules, cricket, swimming, golf, tennis, sailing and boating, basketball, netball, running, skiing and walking. There is really something to appeal to everyone, either to participate in or to watch.

Australian culture

There is no such thing as a 'typical' Australian. There is a wide range of people with social customs, habits and perspectives that might be different from your own. Here are a few tips that might help you acclimatise.

Greetings
Australia is a relatively relaxed and informal place so you might hear people greet each other with a simple 'G'day', 'Hello', 'Hi' or 'How's it going?'. In more formal situations it's most common to greet and complete meetings with a handshake (for both men and women). The same applies for saying 'Goodbye' in a formal setting. In a less formal situation, just saying 'See you later', 'See you around' or 'See ya' is a very common way of completing a goodbye.

Manners
It is customary to say 'please' when you'd like something, regardless of setting and formality. It is also customary that, once you've received something that's been provided you say 'thank you', again regardless of occasion. Australians are very big users of 'Please' and 'Thank you' and it would be interpreted as rudeness if this custom were not observed.

The use of slang
Australians insert slang into daily conversation and it's done almost unconsciously. More examples are listed in the 'Resources' section of our website at www.foreignerincharge.com.

Eye contact

It's customary to engage in direct eye contact with those people talking to you and when you're talking to them. This is seen as a sign of interest and sincerity. Most Australians will make direct eye contact with everyone they meet.

Personal space

Australians like their personal space. About an arm's length is a good distance to converse with someone. Any closer and the person may feel uncomfortable.

Humour

Australians are known for their dry sense of humour involving light-hearted banter, which is commonly known as 'stirring'. It is often a signal of friendship and fun. The style of humour is akin to that of the British and Irish. Irony is used in abundance. Don't worry if you don't understand the humour straightaway; as your knowledge of the country grows you'll be joining in on the laughs.

Socialising in Australia

A lot of socialising in Australia happens in people's homes. You'll be invited to barbecues, dinners or lunches at people's homes and that's very common. Most homes in Australia are relatively large and will often have pools and outdoor spaces that are used for entertaining purposes. The fastest way to get invited to people's homes is to host a party at yours first.

Social invitations

If you receive a verbal or a written invitation to an event it is customary to reply to the host to inform them of your acceptance or to decline. If you're asked to join in or to go on a group social outing, you will be expected to pay for yourself. If you're invited to a friend's house for a meal, it's customary to ask if you can contribute to the meal. This might be something simple, such as bringing a bottle of drink or a platter of food to share (in which case you might be asked to 'bring a plate'). Some parties may be 'BYO', which means you bring your own food or drink. If you are not sure it is perfectly acceptable to check with the host before the event.

Dress code

Dress in Australia tends to be casual. Most workplaces require business attire and will often have a policy outlining the dress requirements.

If an occasion is marked as being 'formal' or requires more formal dress, this will normally be included on the invitation. It is acceptable to check with the host or with the workplace as to the dress requirements.

Coming to live in Australia

What many people expect when they come to live in Australia is that it will be an easy, streamlined transition, particularly if they're coming from a western, English-speaking country. They expect to find Australia a happy, easy-going place where everyone's friendly and assume the inclusion and socialisation will be simple.

The shock many people who are moving to Australia actually find is that, yes, Australians are incredibly friendly and will be very happy to include you and talk to you in a social setting. What they might not do is include you in a closer friendship network.

This will take time as people come to understand you and get to know you. The challenge is, how do you facilitate that? The answer is to become very active and to get involved in things, particularly activities in the school community, sporting clubs or other community or church-based events.

A very helpful strategy is to invite people to join you, and your family, for social events. This can be simple things like attending an event or sporting game, a concert, coffee, a simple meal or picnic. This will demonstrate you are being proactive and that you're interested in other people's company. What you'll find is over time these offers will be reciprocated and, through that ongoing pattern, friendships will build.

Working in Australia
People coming to Australia from a First World English-speaking country might presume the working conditions and strategies that helped make them successful in their previous companies and countries will be easily translated into the Australian context. This might not actually be the case.

While there may be many similarities, there are a number of nuances that often prove to be distinct challenges for new leaders coming into Australia. What most people expect is that Australians will be as humorous, easy-going and fun to get along with in the work context as is portrayed in the social context.

What people aren't always aware of is that Australians can be very sceptical about hierarchy. In the Australian mind, trust and respect are earned not just granted. Australians won't necessarily respect a person or follow their word without question just because they hold a position of hierarchical authority over them. Australians are great ones for wanting to understand 'why?' behind an idea. If this is shared and there is what is perceived to be 'sense' behind the notion, they will more easily support the idea and comply.

3

THE IMPACT ON THE EXPAT FAMILY

You have moved to a new country and a new home, but have you moved your mind? This is a great question to consider when trying to understand the challenge transition brings to expatriates and their families. Most expatriate executives are challenged and excited to be in their new assignment. While this is exciting for them, what is happening with the family who has relocated with them? For many families, the relocation can be viewed as a great imposition rather than a wonderful adventure.

Relocation can create challenging circumstances (particularly for the 'trailing spouse') which are not supported by the standard 'transactional' relocation services provided by most organisations. This chapter explores some of the common experiences of partners and families and provides some strategies and ideas to increase the likelihood of creating an enjoyable experience with wonderful memories.

Given the large demands on the expatriate from the employing organisation, partners and families spend a lot of time by themselves in an unfamiliar environment, cut off from their extended family, friends and known contacts. During this time, they are usually dealing with challenges they have not encountered before (e.g. new school, banking, medical, housing, communications companies and systems), in an unfamiliar environment.

Unintended consequences

If awareness, planning and support are not in place, the result can be an unhappy partner who may (not necessarily consciously) create an environment that negatively affects the performance of the expatriate manager.

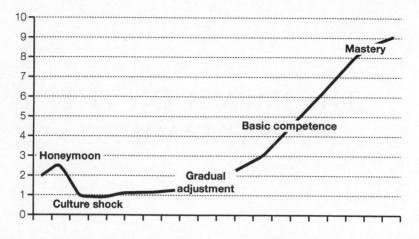

Figure 4: The stages of expatriate adjustment

In fact, one of the most significant factors in the derailment of expatriate assignments is where the partner and/or the family struggle in the transition to their new life and circumstances. Sadly, marriage breakdown is not an uncommon result. Unofficial numbers claim that upwards of 50 per cent of their expatriate marriages fail due to the stress of offshore postings.

Culture shock

It is common for even the most flexible people to endure an initial period of stress when starting their expatriate posting. Commonly known as culture shock, this psychological affliction results when people become anxious and confused in a different environment. In this state, they experience homesickness, depression, irritability and frustration. This experience occurs not only for the expat but for all members of their accompanying family. It can create a very challenging environment and, if not managed, can become a contributor to expatriate failure.

Culture shock is known to move through a number of phases, each of which we will look at.

Phase 1: Honeymoon
The honeymoon phase covers the initial four to six weeks in the new country, and is characterised by the understandable excitement of being in a new country. Everything is new and interesting. It is an adventure.

Phase 2: Culture shock

Once the honeymoon phase is over, culture shock often sets in and can last for six to eight months. Expatriates quickly begin to comprehend the magnitude of the challenges of living and working in a different country. Because nothing is familiar, even the most routine tasks require additional effort.

During this time expats and their families discover that methods and patterns used successfully in previous locations are either worthless or even destructive in another cultural environment. The result can be that you, the expatriate manager, can become distressed, frustrated and ineffective at your job. Then, when you arrive home, you are usually faced with family members who are even more traumatised than you. And each one is expecting to be saved by you, the person responsible for bringing them to this strange country.

The combination of severe adjustments at both work and home results in classic culture shock symptoms: frustration, anger, confusion and a distrust of others. There is no happy place to be during this period. If not recognised and addressed, people can become 'stuck' in this phase and this can be the lasting memory expatriates and their families take with them when they leave the country.

Phase 3: Gradual adjustment

During this phase, which can last from one to two years, expatriates slowly regain their self-confidence and effectiveness in a steady but difficult process. Through trial and error, and by building relationships, they gradually come to understand the need to adapt themselves to the local culture before trying to manage it. Expatriates and their families eventually come to appreciate local customs, cuisine and business practices.

Phase 4: Basic competence

Basic competence in the practices of any country takes years — we estimate this can range from between two to four years from the start of your posting. Despite the challenges, most expatriates are able to develop functional proficiency in the local environment within a couple of years from relocation. In current practice, it is often at this point that an expatriate posting completes. It seems just when people are 'getting the hang of things' it is time to relocate again.

Phase 5: Mastery

For expatriates to make substantial and sustainable progress, they generally need strong relationships with people. This requires a lot of time.

Various studies and experience have shown that at least five to seven years are necessary to develop a deep appreciation of the country and its opportunities.

Understanding the cycles that happen with culture shock is important so there are no surprises as you travel through the various phases. This information can be used to make sure that appropriate planning and action can take place to ensure as smooth a transition as possible.

What is critical here is that most current expat assignments are for three years or less. The challenge is to fast-track through the flux so that you reach mastery in a far shorter timeframe.

Loss of identity

Our work with expatriates and their families demonstrates that one of the greatest challenges faced is usually by the partner, who is often left without a sense of meaning, purpose and identity. This can create great unhappiness and drive unhelpful patterns of behaviour, which negatively impact the family and the expatriate experience.

So much energy and effort is expended on the logistics of the physical move and, while necessary, this can distract from paying attention to the things that will have the most significant impact on psychological well-being, happiness and relationships after the initial flurry of settling in.

What becomes apparent is that in the 'home environment' — the country and city from which you are coming — your partner has an established infrastructure and support network created through years of living in the same community. A significant portion of an individual's personal sense of meaning and value is derived from the roles played and contributions made. This may include work, study, involvement in community, church, charities, sports and schools. The challenge is that, in the new location many of the elements on which your partner depended and formed the basis of their identity may be no longer available.

While some may just take time and effort to re-establish in the new place, challenges such as the loss of identity through working, for example, may not. Many people spend years working at and establishing careers. However, due to visa restrictions it is not unusual for the trailing spouse to be unable to undertake paid work even in their qualified area.

With the move to the new location, the ability to connect with the established mechanisms is weakened through lack of proximity, time zones and sheer opportunity. The power of attachment to, and the fulfilment gained from, these roles cannot be underestimated. There will naturally be a void created.

It can be lonely.

A common issue encountered is finding and establishing relationships and friendships in the new location. Human beings are social by nature. We crave and need companionship and connection with others.

The challenge in an expatriate assignment can be the experience of only having transactional relationships rather than those with depth and meaning. The expatriate experience in Australia is different to that in other geographical areas such as Singapore or Dubai, where the expatriate communities are more obvious in location, in that they live in compounds designed for expatriate living. Therefore, meeting other expatriate families is made easier purely because of accommodation choices. This is not the case in Australia. The choice of where to live is more abundant and often made based on the location of the new workplace.

Experienced trailing spouses will already understand the realisation that in the new location the local people have no need to include you in their lives. They already have full lives with connections and relationships that have been forged over years. They find that, particularly in Australia, people are very friendly but they are not inclusive. They will happily chat, spend time in passing but beyond this they will not necessarily make an effort to include others. As such, expat partners can feel that, in the new location they are only defined by their role in relation to others, for example, chiefly their partner and children. In response, a common pattern is that in the absence of other sources, the emphasis is placed on the expatriate executive partner to provide company and fill the void. This can show up as lots of telephone calls, demands to be home and involved in activities, and lack of flexibility in time.

While you, the working spouse will only want the best for your family, this is a period when you will have multiple demands on your time. Starting a new job is consuming: working in a new company, taking on a new team and being in a new location are all demanding and require effort. All of these things on their own would demand time and attention but in combination the time demands are extraordinary. To then have your family making demands only adds to the challenges.

It's likely you will feel pressure, guilt and responsibility to try to make everyone happy, as you have been the one responsible for uprooting and bringing the family to this new place. It is not unusual for the expat family, particularly the adults, to become very insular and co-dependent. The lack of diversity in this can be stifling for the trailing partner; it can place great pressure on both them and the children.

As a result many expat families become more insular. Sticking together, which is not all bad, often expat families become much closer as the interdependence and reliance on each other for social and emotional support is deepened. But this can also be draining and limiting. Finding trusted caregivers so the adults can have the time and space to be a couple, to mix with other couples and keep their relationship solid can also be something that is sacrificed. Again then, identity is diminished and this can further add to dissatisfaction.

This can create frustration and tension. When not attended to this can result in a spiral where relationships deteriorate and the family environment, often the thing that most people want to maintain, is eroded.

So, what strategies are available for the family to manage in this situation?

Increase awareness and manage expectations

This involves increasing the self-awareness of the family about what is likely to be experienced. With this insight and knowledge it is then possible to make plans to help minimise the impact, recognise tension when it does turn up and quickly take action to address the feelings and situations when they arise.

It can be beneficial to discuss these issues with your partner and family early on, even as part of the decision-making process about moving. A discussion working step by step through the following points can shed light on potentially problematic areas:

- **'What is my current state?'** Discuss and identify the important factors, people and situations that contribute to your partner's sense of identity. Consider both professional and personal contexts, as well any voluntary and community groups and hobbies or leisure activities.
- **New surroundings.** Once the key areas have been noted, look for similar situations in the new country — will there, for example, be opportunities to pursue the same leisure activities or join groups of like-minded people?
- **What is the gap?** Now look for the gaps between what your partner relies on in your home country for their sense of identity and what will be available to them in Australia.
- **Solutions.** How can these gaps possibly be bridged or alternatives identified once you move?

There are a number of ways of doing this process. Excellent resources such as the book *A Portable Identity* can be used as a self-guided tool.[1]

Alternatively, using a mentor or a coach to help test the thinking, realities and pragmatisms of the thinking can be invaluable to establishing a realistic understanding and expectation.

From this base it can be powerful to then be 'forewarned' and therefore proactive about what actions to undertake that will minimise the disturbance and to embed the family into the new location with minimal disruption. There will, of course, be disturbance, but the mindset that there will not be or that it will be minimal is one of the greatest possible issues. Management of expectations is absolutely critical.

Raymond was a successful executive based in Western Europe in a global pharmaceutical company. He had already worked in two leading pharmaceutical organisations and helped set up the affiliate in his own country, which had phenomenal success in its first five years of trading.

He, his pregnant wife and their two young daughters arrived in sunny Sydney, eagerly looking forward to their new adventure. Various problems with accommodation clouded the initial month after arrival but were eventually resolved. The on-boarding program with the organisation did not happen so Raymond just did what he did best — he eagerly 'got on' with the role.

Unfortunately this meant relying on a command-and-control style of leadership coupled with a distant approach towards this staff. A variety of issues occurred and Raymond's performance at work was soon under scrutiny. Coupled with this, his wife, Tanya, had just given birth and was not coping in her new transition, which was also placing huge pressure on Raymond to perform.

Fortunately, Raymond's boss, also an expat, understood the challenges and engaged OSullivanField to work with him. The coach immediately noticed that Raymond was extremely concerned for his wife and family. He was suffering from the 'unhappy wife, unhappy life' syndrome that many expatriate executives experience. The reality of moving to a new country is that it can take up to two years to settle into normality. In this case, Tanya had given birth not long after arriving to Australia and had no immediate family support. She had resorted to calling Raymond every two hours at work to debrief the latest news on the baby.

With the support of his coach, Raymond encouraged Tanya to reach out for the local 'mother's group', the support of which provided an alternative network and alleviated her need to contact Raymond so often. He also arranged his work schedule so that he could arrive at work a little later in the mornings in order to take his older two children to school, thus allowing his wife to focus on the new baby. Finding ways to manage his home life left Raymond some space to consider how he might lead differently in Australia and turn around the negative impressions that were building of him.

4

LEADING IN AUSTRALIA

The topic of leadership is very broad and this section is not designed to cover every aspect but rather to give a thumbnail sketch as a guide for prospective leaders coming to Australia.

As in many countries, leaders in Australia are admired and despised for a range of reasons. Australians value leaders who are able, talented and promoted for the best reasons. They value leaders who are able to give *context* in terms of why decisions are being made and *content* in terms of what the followers need to do in order to achieve organisational outcomes. Respect for leaders is accorded due to ability rather than position or title. While nepotism is an issue in other countries, it is generally not a problem in Australia, as at a society level meritocracy is valued. Broadly speaking, Australia has an issue with ageism and young leaders are favoured. Given the overall population is ageing rapidly, this will become a potential issue down the track.

Initially, Australians will be very friendly and interested in hearing about where you have come from, your country of origin, your family, where you will live and, of course, your thoughts about Australia. However, Australians will reserve judgement on your *capability* as the leader. Whether this Australian trait comes from the history of rebellion, when convicts forged the country, or the sheer sense of practicality that pervades the nation, the idea that leaders need to prove themselves abounds.

Leaders who are successful in Australia seem to embody a range of complementary leadership traits and styles. These involve:

- the ability to give clear direction while valuing teamwork
- adhering to ethics while maintaining a sense of creativity and innovation

- having extensive ability in one's particular field while not coming across as a complete expert
- being formal in terms of having strong processes to achieve outcomes yet being informal in a personal leadership approach.

Leaders in Australia do not generally seek overt material possessions as a sign of their leadership, such as executive dining rooms and bathrooms. Quite often senior leaders sit in an open plan office and share floor space with their direct reports.

Decision making

Given that senior leaders are paid to make decisions it is worthwhile adding a comment on decision making in Australia. Broadly speaking, Australia is egalitarian in its outlook and individual input is sought as part of a consultation process. At an organisation level, Australians are very happy for senior leaders to lead the decision-making process in accordance with company policy but do enjoy being consulted as part of that overall process. Initially this may seem to be slowing down fast decisions, but it is worthwhile adhering to a consultation process, at least in the initial stages of leadership.

As a general rule, Australians are analytical and objective. Achieving results is seen to be more important than saving face. Profit is generally more important than market share. Adhering to the overall rules and regulations of society organisation is more important than a leader winning at all costs. Generally speaking, logic is valued over emotion. Australians can be seen to be blunt but this is because they generally have no problem saying no to something. Being direct is valued and therefore there is little point in evasiveness. Australians value leaders making decisions and often get frustrated when a new leader is seen to delay the decision-making process or is perceived to not back the decisions that are made. A wishy-washy leader who is seen to be indecisive or who can be influenced to change their mind by many different types of people is considered to be the least desirable leader in Australia.

Negotiating

Australia does not have a history of bartering as in Asian and Middle Eastern societies. Therefore, Australians, by nature, negotiate for a win–win and expect the first offer to be relatively close to the final offer. Negotiations that are over-enthusiastic or deemed to be hyper-filled usually provoke resistance and indeed sarcasm from locals. Vendors and suppliers who are openly derogatory about their competition or the industry they work in are viewed as being less than professional and often not taken seriously. Australians tend to say what they mean and therefore expect to be taken literally. It follows, then, for you to mean what you say as they will take you literally. Superiority is not valued as this is a country that values 'the battler' (the underdog).

While relationships are very important in Australia, using this to one's advantage does not necessarily guarantee a win during negotiation. In some countries, being related to a key decision maker is almost a guarantee for the decision to be made in one's favour. With some notable and often notorious exceptions, this is not the case in Australia. One local distinction that may seem unusual is the use of irony and humour. Newcomers to Australia have to learn to listen to what is being said and to read between the lines to understand to what degree a person is being direct versus giving feedback through humour.

Once negotiations have been concluded the rubber stamping on the administration side of the deal may take longer than expected. This is particularly true when dealing with state and federal governments.

Delegating and supervising

Australians are by nature laid-back and do not like layers of hierarchy. Most organisations strive for as flat a structure as is possible. Many leadership teams use the fact that Australia is a long way from head office (wherever head office actually is) to enable a flat structure to take place. Therefore there is a need for leaders to ensure greater accountability at individual and team level in the organisation. Australians like to understand the context for strategy and major decisions and, as much as is possible, to be involved in the decision-making process in a consultative approach. While Australians understand and respect various levels of leadership and understand that some decisions are made at particular levels, as much as possible they want to be involved or at least informed.

In a later chapter I outline various communication platforms you can use in order to keep staff fully informed of the progress the organisation is making. A new leader to Australia needs to be able to delegate and empower their staff to take action on important items. Once Australians feel they understand the context in which their role fits, they are very happy to take full responsibility to deliver. Of course, this may vary at individual levels but, broadly speaking, Australians are happy to be held accountable.

For leaders coming from more formal cultures such as the United Kingdom, Australians can initially appear frustratingly laid-back. This can often be deceiving, as the laid-back approach does not mean a 'do not achieve' approach. In fact, many leaders who come to Australia comment upon their departure three years later that Australians have figured out how to best balance the way to do work and the way to do life in general. Supervision and delegation should be managed in a collaborative way and public confrontation or public dress-downs should be avoided at all costs. While in an Asian context this may lead to an executive losing face, in an Australian context the leader who is doing the dressing-down is viewed as 'up themselves'. Taking a superior approach is seen to be distasteful in Australia.

How to make a good impression

Australians value leaders who are confident, down-to-earth, authentic and relatively direct. There is little fanfare involved in settling most issues and Australians tend to go about their business and get the job done without undue stress. Leaders command respect by being competent in their sphere of experience, by being relatively open to new ideas and asking for input, but also by being confident enough to back their own decisions once they are made. The number of expats coming to Australia seems to increase every year as global expatriation programs increase. Therefore, some organisations will have experienced a never-ending cycle of expats coming through for their experience 'down-under'. This may lead to a sense of cynicism or even the locals being jaded by the latest expat leader. Do not buy into this as Australians are very happy to be led by an expat leader who is confident and capable.

Despite a sense of informality, Australians do have a stronger sense of formality in business relationships. Cold calling or dropping in unannounced is unusual. Making appointments to visit someone at their office or to meet them for coffee is more normal. For executives coming from overseas, the ability to meet people for coffee meetings seems to be easier in Australia than their experiences elsewhere. Indeed, many overseas visitors have commented that all business in Sydney and Melbourne seems to be done in cafés.

Turning up to meetings and turning up on time is essential. Being five minutes late is acceptable as long as the person has phoned ahead to suggest they will not be on time. Leaders who come from the parts of the globe where punctuality is not considered important underestimate the poor impression they can create in Australia when they regularly turn up late for meetings. This is deemed to be disrespectful for the locals. When scheduling appointments it is important to be aware of the main holiday breaks in Australia as the locals are very good at taking holidays. The summer holidays run from late December to February and this coincides with school and university breaks. Most executives will take a minimum of two weeks off during this time period. Other major holidays occur around the Anzac Day holiday time in late April, the Easter break and in winter between June and July. Most business hours are 8.30 a.m. to 5.30 p.m. Depending on seniority, some executives are very happy to meet before or after these hours but it is worthwhile checking before assuming.

Forms of address

As mentioned, Australians are generally informal and friendly. Common greetings are 'Hello' and 'Hi' and occasionally 'G'day'. For a visitor, saying 'G'day' is deemed to be in good humour for major presentations or one-off meetings; however, using the phrase on a regular basis may be considered patronising. Both men and women shake hands at the beginning of meetings and at the end. Occasionally men and women who know each other relatively well are happy to kiss on the cheeks as a form of greeting similar to the French and other cultures. Men rarely kiss each other in public unless they're from Greek or Italian origins. When writing someone's name the salutation is usually formal such as 'Mr', 'Mrs' or 'Ms'. Other titles, such as 'Dr' or 'Professor', are used regularly. Ironically, when someone insists they are addressed by their title they can be seen to be 'up themselves'.

Dress sense

Generally speaking, business wear in Australia is dictated by the particular industry. As an example, the dress code for those working in financial industries such as banking or insurance is as traditional as in other countries. Men are expected to wear suits, shirts and ties and women are expected to dress formally.

Other industries are less formal and more casual. The weather will also affect the degree to which people can dress up, particularly in the summer time. In the capital cities people will still wear shirts and potentially ties during the summer but in cities such as Brisbane, or Darwin in the Northern Territory, where the humidity is very high, most people wear short-sleeved shirts and shorts. The term 'smart casual' usually refers to wearing jeans or long casual pants and a shirt or polo shirt.

Top ten essential things to know about Australia

Here's a recap of the top ten things you should know about leading in Australia.

1. Australia is big. As a land mass it is on par with India and the United States but as a population size it is dwarfed by those countries. It is a diverse, multicultural society.
2. Australians are generally informal and prefer a laid-back, casual approach to most things. This does not mean that they are not productive or high performing, but the approach appears casual.
3. Australians value authenticity and sincerity. The phrase 'Show us who you really are' is often used.
4. Australians are very down-to-earth and are certainly pragmatists more than theorists. While conceptual thinking is important, how your ideas will be turned into reality is far more important. Australians are friendly but are deceivingly direct. They are open and approachable but also quite explicit. For leaders coming from countries where politeness is the norm, you may be surprised at how direct Australians can be. This is not to be confused with aggression.
5. Following on from the point above, taking a direct approach, being prompt, being focused and succinct are qualities that are admired in Australia.
6. Humour is often used to deflect attention, to create relaxed atmospheres and to build out presentations. Likewise, Australians tend to shorten people's names out of humour and affection: Samuel becomes Sam, Jonathan becomes Jon and my name, Padraig, is now 'Pod'.
7. 'Give the battler a go' is a phrase you may hear. This speaks to Australians' sense of fair play. In a debate or argument make sure you are well reasoned and logical when putting forward your side of the story. Trying to win based upon authority is not well received.
8. Sport is usually the answer to all issues. Whether it be rugby union, rugby league, soccer or Australian Rules (all of which are regarded as footy), sport usually has the answer to most things.

9. Australians are passionate about their country. Many nations have this trait but Australians do not necessarily overtly show this in the way Americans do. However, beneath the surface Australians believe that this is 'the lucky country' for good reasons.

10. Australia is big and a long way from everywhere. The best and worst side of Australia is its distance from everywhere else. Therefore, when travelling overseas to/from Australia, be considerate of jet lag as well as the time it takes to re-acclimatise to other time zones.

PART 2

PALDER — A FRAMEWORK FOR EXPATRIATE LEADERSHIP

5

INTRODUCING THE PALDER FRAMEWORK

In his book *The First 90 Days*, Michael Watkins lays out what has become a well-respected framework in helping leaders transition into a new role.[1] His premise is that the new leader needs to accomplish particular tasks within the first 90 days to be set up for success from that point forward. George Bradt and his colleagues lay out a more detailed transition plan for new leaders in the book *The New Leader's 100-Day Action Plan*.[2] Both these books provide useful frameworks for leaders transitioning into a new role. However, expatriate leaders have nuances in their transition that make their experience unique. As such, our experience is that a 90- or a 100-day plan is not enough to 'set them up for success'.

In this book we outline an integrated framework, designed and utilised by OSullivanField, mapping out the six different transition phases an expatriate leader will undergo in the first twelve to 24 months of leadership. It illustrates the waves of change the leader, their family and the organisation will undergo as the new leader takes their position. Within each phase we outline how the expat leader can successfully navigate and what models of leadership they can draw upon to help them do so. The key events that typically take place within each transition phase are highlighted and there are also tips, checklists and key points to consider. In each of these events there are underlying skills required to facilitate the transition through the event. Each skill is clearly explained and translated into the context in which it will need to be applied (e.g. individual, team and organisation levels). Finally, the key outputs you will need to deliver at each phase are documented.

I have previously outlined the causes contributing to the significant failure rate of expatriate leaders. The complexity of transitions they undergo lead them to either making substandard decisions, leading in a culturally inappropriate way, or having family or spousal issues that detract from their success. Our experience has been that, by having a fully integrated approach in supporting the new leader in their transition the likelihood of success is increased two- to threefold.

Many organisations do offer support, be it limited in some cases and well intentioned in most. At most, minimal support is limited to relocation services to the country and into a home locally. Effectively this has the impact of implying 'we got you here now carry on'! On-boarding programs to the local organisation work well in helping the new leader understand the physical location they are working in and how the security systems work. Cultural on-boarding programs serve to educate the new expat on local culture and how it differs from their country of origin. Many organisations offer a traditional executive coaching program to support the new leader, which may focus on leadership transitions in a similar way to supporting a leader who has been promoted internally.

An embedded program similar to the 'Expat Program' offered by OSullivanField is a customised program that involves a structured on-boarding program to the organisation and role, cultural learning spread over twelve months and a customised executive coaching program that addresses the exact issues expats typically face when relocating to a new country or assignment. The combination of all these areas has a positive, cascading benefit effect, which increases the chances of a successful assignment.

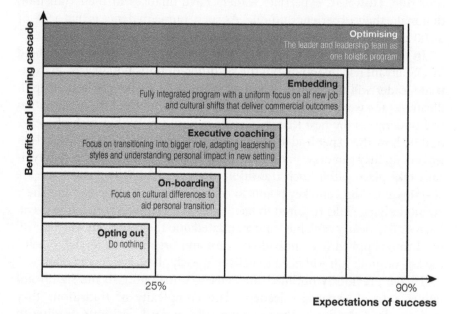

Figure 5: The cascading benefits of a structured expatriate support program

The PALDER framework

There are six major transition phases associated with the expat leadership role. These make up the PALDER model, as seen in Figure 6: pre-arrival; arrival; look, listen and learn; decide; energise; review and renew. Each phase is visible from a timeline perspective and tends to follow typical timelines. For the purpose of this book we have outlined the typical timelines we have experienced with our clients. It is also common for these periods to overlap. They have been kept discrete in the model for ease of illustration. However, these are not mandatory and we recognise every executive and situation will have its own unique perspective.

We'll now look at each phase in the PALDER framework; following this will be chapters exploring each of these phases in greater detail.

Phase 1: Pre-arrival

This phase is predominately consumed with the executive being considered for the new role, interviewing and negotiating when the offer is made. The transition starts here. Being considered for a new expatriate role implies the candidate has already been successful within the organisation. The fact they have performed well in some role means more senior leaders in the same organisation believe they are capable of taking on an expatriate role elsewhere in the organisation.

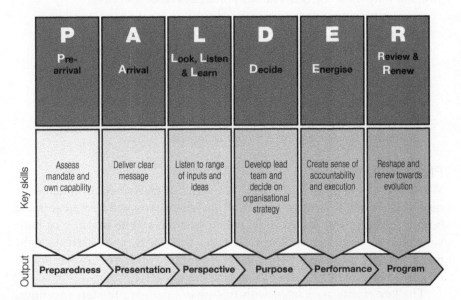

Figure 6: PALDER — A framework for expatriate leadership

It is very easy during transitions to lose confidence in your own ability. In fact, most human beings lose confidence in themselves on a regular basis. The concept of 'imposter syndrome' — i.e. 'I am not good enough at this job and someday soon somebody is going to find that out …' — is alive and well within the minds of many expatriate leaders. Remembering you have been successful somewhere is a great reminder of why you have been chosen for this job.

Some key events that happen during this phase include the accepting and negotiating of the final offer of the new role; visiting the new country, often with your partner, to meet and greet the locals and make the final decision to accept the role; organising the announcement of the promotion and departure; setting the pre-start and the start dates; understanding the mandate the new leadership role will require; and self-assessing and preparing for the new role.

The key skill associated with this phase is understanding history. This includes history in terms of your own capability and how you assess your own potential, strengths and derailers against the new role. At an organisational level, understanding the history of the position offered and learning the mandate you will inherit with this new position is crucial.

Preparedness for the role is vital in navigating this transition well. Preparation at this time also refers to the mental preparations of your partner and family, who are about to undertake this new adventure with you and may have concerns about potential loss of identity.

> *When Chris was struggling in his new role nine months after arrival, his coach reminded him to consider his previous successes. Somewhere in his career he had to have been successful, otherwise the organisation would not have deemed him capable of taking on this role. Prompted by his coach, Chris wrote down a list of reasons why the organisation had considered him. Doing this exercise helped to re-validate the reasons for him being chosen.*

Phase 2: Arrival

While the arrival phase is the one that is full of excitement and nervousness, it also often feels the most daunting. Ideally, you will have negotiated both a pre-start and a start date, which will allow time to settle in both yourself and your family. Depending on their ages, your arrival might mean nothing particularly for infants or young children, however it can be quite daunting for older or teenage children.

The key events associated with this phase include pre-start meetings, preparing for the first day, key stakeholder meetings, the new leader assimilation meeting, developing a transition plan, developing three-, six- and twelve-month plans and, of course, settling in your family.

There are two key skills associated with this transition:

- **Self-management.** This is crucial. Your ability to centre yourself while all the eyes of the organisation are upon you on your first day and first week is very important. The 'executive presence' you exude, or not, will be the talking point in many lunch meetings and informal conversations in the organisation. Positive first impressions are critical. You never get a second chance to make a first impression.
- **Clear messaging.** Both at a direct-reports and at a wider organisation level it is critical that you convey a clear message about yourself and other important matters on the first day and in the first week. Preparation and deliberate wording is essential. We offer frameworks and a new leader assimilation model to help you master this activity.

The key output for this phase is the *presentations* you deliver in your first days in the organisation. Many of the questions that naturally exist when a new leader comes into an organisation will be answered quickly and a sense of confidence is developed by the way you portray yourself.

Phase 3: Look, listen and learn

This is one of the most important phases in the transition of an expatriate leader. The waves of change increase dramatically as you now take the reins of the new role. This phase tends to officially start at the end of week 1 and continues to approximately week 10. In many cases, once the announcement has been made about taking the role, as the new leader you begin actively learning everything you can and preparing to start that new role. However, many expatriate leaders lay the foundations for their failure during this phase. They hugely underestimate the importance of taking time to fully understand the organisation, its culture, operating environment, and industry environment and to ask pertinent questions before making assumptions.

Janet had been in the organisation for five months when the HR Director took her aside and suggested the leadership team would like to do a review with her on her first five months. The HR Director suggested they bring in an external experienced facilitator to ensure no question was left unanswered and all views were surfaced professionally. Janet initially thought this to be a strange request but was happy to proceed, assuming the feedback would be positive.

The facilitator set up interviews with Janet, the HR Director and all of their peers and came back a week later to facilitate a session between Janet and her peers together. Having conducted many of these sessions in the past, his style was professional yet honest, transparent and direct. He had a clear message for Janet: 'You are not listening. You have not listened since the day you came here. We appreciate your very strong commercial acumen, however if you continue not to listen you will be leading a leadership team that has no confidence in you.'

Understandably, Janet was shocked. Through careful facilitation she learnt that by not seeking to understand what the leadership team had done previously, she was often making incorrect assumptions. By suggesting a clear direction forward without understanding the prior organisational strategies, she was insulting the leadership team by assuming their lack of ability and also making grave mistakes in her strategic decisions.

Thankfully, Janet listened to the feedback.

The major events associated with this transition include Key Influencer's meetings (called the KI meets), functional sit-ins, doing some 'missionary work', assessments of direct reports, assessing organisational culture and doing a 'Be-Do-Get' process (called the BDG process) with your family. These are explained on the website.

At an individual level, the essential skills needed in this transition are listening and learning at a local level. Understanding what happens within the new country and how your personal leadership style needs to adapt to the environment cannot be underestimated. The next leadership skill is at the team level. You need to understand how the local leadership team operates, how it makes decisions, how it leads the organisation and what kind of leadership input the team needs from their new leader.

Finally, the ability to develop a range of perspectives is crucial. The fact you are coming from another country is a huge benefit. This naturally brings an international perspective, which, if deployed well, can be of benefit to the local organisation. Combined with this, as part of the next phase, you need to gain perspective from outside of the organisation at a national level. This means meeting with other industry players, fellow peers, industry associations, political stakeholders and other influencers. An ability to elevate your thinking to include many perspectives is important. In their book *The Leadership Pipeline*, authors Ram Charan, Stephen Drotter and James Noel suggest this transition is possibly the most difficult of leadership thinking transitions. This transition (level 4 transition in Figure 7) to a business manager role such as a GM or MD level, requires you to actually change the way you think. With the change in role comes an increase in complexity, visibility, impact and a decrease in support from other leaders. Being able to actively seek out a range of perspectives is an important factor in fully understanding the issues at hand.

There are two main outputs from this phase that will set the leader up for ongoing success. First is honouring and understanding the past. One of the most commonly cited grievances organisations have regarding new expatriate leaders is that, upon their arrival, the new leader casts negative aspersions on everything that has happened before. It is almost as if they have an attitude of 'you should be grateful I am here to save you from all of your mistakes'! The leader needs to remember that this is the same leadership team who is responsible for whatever has happened in the past. While there might have been mistakes, there are also undoubtedly successes and reasons for likely success.

The second key output is integrating knowledge from all inputs, staff, job reports, customers, stakeholders and other collaboration points to

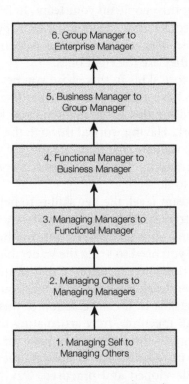

Figure 7: Levels of management transition[3]

develop an integrated perspective of the current reality. Building up perspectives that describe the organisation in terms of where it is today, the environment it is operating in, the issues it is facing, feedback from customers and staff all go towards helping you create a clear picture of the future strategy and the role your new leadership will play in creating that strategy.

Phase 4: Decide

Typically this phase starts at around weeks 6 to 12 and can stretch to as far as week 14. During this phase, the feeling of change decreases for the first time since arrival. This is often expressed as the point where 'I start to feel like I know what I'm doing in my new role'. It is at this point you start to make some key decisions and feel you are now doing the job you were brought in to do.

The events typical of this phase include the leadership team mandate session, strategy work-up sessions, 'paint the lobby' projects, communication plans, town hall announcements and cascade meetings. These are all discussed in this chapter. It is also during this phase you will be making up your mind about the people on your team. In his famed book *Good to Great*, Jim Collins spoke about having the right people on the bus. The reality is that most leaders inherit their bus passengers and need time to figure out whether they are the right ones.

There are three core skills in this phase you need to either develop or utilise. You need to have a clear sense of what the organisation needs to do. The springboard for this is the mandate you have understood from your pre-arrival work. Having worked through the 'look, listen and learn' phase, you can now validate that mandate or vary your original thinking from the new information. The leader needs to be clear as to what the organisation needs to do.

At a leadership team level, the key skill is to help the leadership team decide the overall strategy. They may have already been given a mandate and therefore you and your leadership team will have to execute that. In most cases, though, you need to bring the leadership team with you in the evaluation, deliberation and execution of that strategy.

At an organisation level, the key skill is that you be seen to lead, to set the course and be visible in the articulation of this new journey. Speaking well at town hall meetings, fully articulating the reason for the new mandate and strategy or the evolution of prior strategies is essential for organisational buy-in. The ability to answer questions from the floor often needs to be developed and practised. Developing your executive presence to ensure confidence as the organisational figurehead is one of the key hallmarks of successful leadership transitions. Many leaders fail at this point.

The overarching output for the leader, the leadership team and the organisation at this stage is a sense of direction and leadership. The leadership team needs to feel confident and committed to the shared purpose and direction. The overall organisation needs to feel the leaders are clear about the direction and have confidence in their ability to lead.

Phase 5: Energise

Typically this starts at week 12 and continues up to week 20. The challenges of change kick back in as you are faced with the reality of executing your mandate as new leader. You will face pockets of resistance from parts of the business you least expect. They will question your ability and bring home the reality of leading in a new country in ways you could not have predicted before arrival.

It is often at this stage that your family are feeling culture shock as they face the stark reality of 'we don't know many people here, we are alone'. School-aged children are faced with the reality of breaking into new friendship groups and often yearn for their old friends from the home country. Your partner has set up home, sorted out the furniture, set up most of the services including electricity, water, banking services and the like and has volunteered for as many school and other committees as possible. They are now starting to wonder what their new life will feel like from this point forward. Skype becomes the tool of choice in the evening time as they try and fill the void of a lack of familiar relationships in the new country with those from the old.

For many expatriate leaders this phase is a very difficult one. They are settling into the role and starting to face resistance and their family is often starting to feel uncomfortable in their new environment. The overall adventure is not quite as exciting as it might have been! Our experience with working alongside expat leaders is that this is the second most common phase when they make their mistakes.

The major events that typically take place in this phase include commencing the leadership team on a high-performance journey, reviewing the organisational culture and identity (and re-setting this if required), and reviewing the organisation's overall accountability. Events also include making decisions on the appropriateness of members of the executive leadership team and taking action if required, having a transition review with the leadership team and your own boss, who may well be in another country. Finally, this is the time to check in with your family to see how they are going in their transition.

There are two distinct and crucial skill sets in this phase. At an individual level, you need to 'oscillate your energy'. This is a phrase stemming from sporting psychology and describes how athletes have to manage their energy levels to ensure performance at critical times. Given how ambitious executives naturally are, particularly expatriate leaders, many burn themselves out by attempting to continually sustain peak performance levels in the first six months. The role demands you be at your most energetic during this and the next phase.

Leaders need to learn or relearn habits and rituals that lead to sustained performance to ensure they are the most energetic while leading the organisation.

At a team level, the key skill is for you to execute. This means holding and being seen to hold the leadership team accountable for doing what they have committed themselves to. If a change of culture is needed to move towards one where accountability is paramount, this will only happen if the leadership team are themselves held accountable. Similarly, the skill at an organisation level is execution and therefore this accountability mindset and behaviour needs to cascade through the organisation.

As obvious as it may seem, the output at this stage is co-designing a road map to and leading the charge to achieve *performance.*

Phase 6: Review and renew

The last, albeit the longest, phase is called 'review and renew'. This tends to start at around week 24 and continues to eighteen to 24 months. As the name suggests, the key context for this phase involves reviewing the organisation and progress to date, reshaping where needed and constantly renewing the energy required to achieve the objectives.

The key events during this phase include the leadership team's journey towards high performance; refining the leadership team's operating rhythm; organisational rhythms such as quarterly business review processes; and adapting or adopting a culture development program for the organisation.

In terms of key skills, you need to play the long game. This means holding the focus of what is important for the organisation, how aligned the organisation is to the mandate and what you, as leader, need to continue to do to make sure you are leading effectively. This will need to be done in the face of challenge — the challenges (and possibly resistance) of a relocated family, from an organisation that has a new leader and, particularly, the challenges of being in a country with an unfamiliar culture.

At a leadership team level, the key skill is adaptability. This means continually reviewing progress, barriers to success, team performance and individual performance throughout the organisation. The ability to do all this will lead to the first organisational skill: building organisational performance through a series of programs and over time giving the organisation a distinct market advantage. The continual performance will be moderated by the organisation's starting point and at what phase of development it was in when the leader arrived.

The ultimate output of this phase is continued evolution or revolution, depending on where the organisation started. Typically, the visual representation of this is achieved through a series of *programs* that the organisation runs to underpin continued performance. Success during this phase will reflect positively on the expatriate leader, and after their contract (which typically lasts three years) they would be offered a new assignment elsewhere. However, as we have said before, the failure rate can be between 25 to 40 per cent. Our experience is the closer the leader sticks to an integrated program like this, the more likely they are to succeed and to be offered an exciting new challenge.

6

THE PRE-ARRIVAL PHASE

Skills needed

At an individual level, understand your own history and capability to assess against the mandate for the new role.

At the organisational level, understand the organisation's local history to make sense of the mandate.

Key question

What do I need to find out to ensure I am ready?

Key outcome

Preparedness.

Susan received a phone call from her boss, Bill, in Boston. He was calling to give her the heads-up that at a meeting the next day she was going to be considered for the new role of GM for the Australian affiliate based in Sydney. He wanted her to be ready to receive a phone call from the Vice President of International Operations, who was due to contact her in the next couple of days to ask about her interest. 'From now on in Susan, you need to be getting ready for the new role in Australia,' Bill said to her.

Susan was both excited at the prospect — as this was something she had been aiming for — but also nervous, as it would mean relocating her family from Chicago for the first time. 'What would you advise that I do?' she asked of Bill. 'Well, first of all, you have to get the role,' he replied, almost laughing, 'then negotiate the terms and consider what you have to do before relocating. From my experience the next six weeks will set you up for success or not, depending on how well you manage yourself. Let me know when you have an interview with José from International and let's sit down and plan for that.'

It makes absolute sense that being considered for an international role is the first step in actually acquiring it. In most sophisticated multinational organisations, the 'high performing talent' map is drawn up long in advance of positions becoming available. Usually on a six-monthly basis, senior leaders are asked to assess their direct reports against performance and potential grids. International assignments are often considered six months to two years in advance of positions becoming available, as these roles are critical for the long-term success of the organisation.

First-time expatriate roles are given priority consideration due to the location difficulties and the high failure rates, described in other chapters. Many executives fail to understand that being considered for a role does not actually mean being offered the role. Most of the executives will go through an interview process to be considered and then are offered a location visit to the new country before the negotiations for the role actually start. At every stage of this process it is imperative for the executive to 'sell themself' and to make sure they are getting ready to take up the role before they actually decide to accept an offer. The phrase 'sell before you buy' is an important one to be mindful of for potential expatriate leaders.

The chart overleaf outlines some key questions you may be asked and reasons for the organisation to ask these questions. As with any selling process, a great salesperson outlines the benefits as opposed to just the features of whatever they are selling. When you are selling an intangible such as your ability to take on a new role elsewhere, it is critical to understand the motivations behind the question and address the benefits to the organisation of choosing you.

The three key areas for which an executive needs to prepare answers are: personal and leadership strengths; personal and family motivations; and cultural fit. One multi-study report suggests three key outcomes which, if achieved, will work towards ensuring the expatriate's success. They are:

- intercultural relationship effectiveness
- cultural adjustment, including family adjustment
- tasks that ensure job performance.[1]

There are over 30 different instruments available to measure and prepare for expatriate readiness but they all measure similar things. Research from these instruments suggest the four most important skills correlating with success are spouse and family communication, the ability to set expectations, interpersonal interests and open-mindedness.[2] The Overseas Assessment Inventory (OAI) suggests there are fourteen significant

Table 1: Potential interview questions

Interview questions	Reason for asking/focus area for investigation
Describe an ideal subordinate. Tell me about the last person you fired. Why? What would you do differently next time? What perceptions do employees have of you? How have you improved subordinates' performance? How have you developed as a leader in the last three years? What did you learn from your last appraisal/360 review/assessment? To what degree have you developed subordinates who have been promoted to other executive positions? What do you look for when hiring people? What techniques have you used to build team morale? How did you build the last team you led? How have you supported the weaker members of your group? How have you developed strategy and implemented that?	Personal and leadership strengths
Talk me through your involvement in any recent turnaround situations. Talk me through your involvement in a recent penetration of a new market. Talk me through your involvement in a recent handling of a start-up situation. Talk me through your involvement in a recent difficult budgeting exercise. Talk me through your involvement in a recent policy creation/decision. If Google were running our business what would they do? Given the explosion of the internet 2.0, what impacts do you see for our products/services?	Intellectual capital (one's global understanding, cosmopolitan outlook and general cognitive complexity)
How do you believe you generally contribute in group discussions? What makes you effective person-to-person or in small groups? What accomplishments can you tell me about to show you are a good communicator? How do you rate yourself as a presenter?	Influencing in general (individuals, groups and systems unlike one's own to achieve strategic goals and objectives)

Interview questions	Reason for asking/focus area for investigation
How do you go about selling your ideas? Why? Where are the improvements needed? How did you handle the last rejection in business you received? How do you learn who are the decision makers/influencers etc.? Give an example. How would you improve your general communications skills? Describe some of your presentations. From whom have you sought advice in the last five years? Last month? Last week? For whom are you a mentor?	Influencing in general (cont.)
What might your closest personal friend say they disliked about you? What is your greatest strength? Weakness? What can you do for us that another candidate could not do? How would you describe your personality? How do you learn? What excites you? Where do you get creative input from (e.g. books, art, photography etc.). What has been the favourite holiday you went on? Why?	Psychological capital (one's passion for diversity, quest for adventure and overall self-assurance)
What was your most recent 360-degree feedback/assessment centre/appraisal trying to tell you? If you have worked with an executive coach, what were they trying to help you with? Success levels? What feedback have you received from peers? What mistakes did you make in your last assignment? Why? What would you do again? What brick walls have you encountered? How did you get around them? What was your most difficult leadership moment? Why? What traits/habits have you dropped over time as you have matured as a leader? Who do you reach out to for help when needed? What external support have you developed over time? What internal mentors have you fostered over time?	Levels of feedback received (resources and support to help you learn from the experiences you've had; how you demonstrate levels of flexibility, which manifests as ability to act differently in different situations and contexts)

Table 1: Potential interview questions

Interview questions	Reason for asking/focus area for investigation
Where are you now in your career and where will you be in three years?	Personal and family motivations
What are your short-term objectives? Long-term?	
What is the best aspect of your current position? The worst?	
What interests you most about the position we are discussing? The least?	
What factors would lead you to leave your present position?	
What aspects of your previous positions have you liked/disliked?	
What overseas travel have you/family done together?	
What plans do you have for your children's schooling?	
Do you have friends who are expats? Their experiences?	
What are your plans to stay in touch with family?	
Do you have plans for your spouse to work abroad?	
Previous interactions with people of different gender orientation, religion and cultures? What happened?	Social capital (one's intercultural empathy, interpersonal impact and general diplomacy)
What surprises have you had when working with people from different cultures? What did you learn?	
Experience of leading virtual cross-cultural teams?	
How do you recognise the rights and expectations of shareholders, employees, customers, suppliers and the wider community?	Integrity and issues abroad
How do you handle trade-offs? When were you put into a situation where you had to decide between the overt right thing to do versus an easy or expedient thing?	
When have you had to question advisors such as accountants, bankers and lawyers on matters of integrity?	

skills an expatriate leader needs to develop or have before departure. They include intercultural effectiveness, expectations, open-mindedness, respect for others' beliefs, trusting people, tolerance, personal control, flexibility, patience, adaptability, self-confidence, interpersonal interests, interpersonal harmony and spouse and family communication.

In preparing for the interview, you need to understand that the questions will be geared towards uncovering your competencies in these areas. Behavioural interviewing as a technique is built upon the premise that both past success and the ability to explain past success will predict future success. However, we know with expatriate relocations that many expatriate leaders are undergoing five different transitions for the first time and therefore past successes in many cases do not predict future success. The ability to develop the skills as outlined earlier is imperative.

Visiting Australia for the first time

When Susan went home to tell her husband, Joe, she had the opportunity to go to Australia and take on a new role he was quite excited. They had always talked about going overseas as a family and hopefully having an adventure in the process. Given her seniority in the organisation both Susan and her husband were aware of many colleagues who had gone on expatriate assignments, and some had enjoyed them while others had not.

Joe was very keen to visit Sydney to have a look before they decided as a family to take on the role. They organised for Joe's parents to mind their two young children for ten days while they spent time travelling to Sydney, exploring the city and trying to get an understanding of what their new life may be like. Susan's boss, Bill, had suggested to her that ensuring Joe would be happy with the new city was an essential part of her due diligence before she finally accepted the role. Bill shared with her his personal experience of living overseas with his wife, who was very unhappy in a particular country. This eventually led to a marriage breakdown. Bill clearly did not wish this to happen to Susan.

The first visit to Australia, or any other country where you are being sent, is important on many levels. It gives you a first meeting with some of your direct reports, particularly the local Human Resources Director and Executive Assistant. The local office no longer becomes an image on an organisation map but is brought to life by walking around the building and getting a sense of how it feels.

Meeting real estate agents who specialise in expatriate locations gives a tangible sense to the research you will have already done from your home country. Meeting with school principals gives you a very solid feel of what the school system would be like for your children. And from a living perspective, you and your spouse can get a sense of what it would be like to live there. Even though on the initial trip you are more akin to a tourist on a short visit to a holiday destination, with an active outlook you will begin to form an understanding of the realities of daily life in Sydney, Melbourne or other Australian cities.

Visiting the office

In most organisations the international head office will liaise with the local Human Resource Director to organise the visit of a prospective new General Manager/Managing Director. Details such as flights, arrival times, pick-ups, hotel accommodation will all be organised locally and, given the visit includes the prospective new leader, most human resource directors are keen for the visit to be a success.

The variables of visiting the office include, of course, whether the existing business leader is still in place and also the reasons for their imminent departure. It is ideal to have a half-day meeting with the existing business leader to understand the business and its people. At this stage a temptation may well be to dig deep into the details of the business; however, the role has not yet been secured and the maxim 'sell before you buy' still applies.

Just as you are gauging and getting a feel for the new location and business, so too will the local staff be doing the same with their potential new leader. In mature economies like Australia, the local Human Resource Director is often involved in the hiring of international executives to the country and their opinion is valued at a regional or international level. Remembering that, even at this early stage, the local Human Resource Director is a potential ally is useful for expatriate leaders on their due diligence visit. Building up a relationship even before the role is offered will go a long way to ensuring success upon arrival into the country.

Accommodation

The biggest question for every expatriate leader is: where will my family live and will they be happy in this new country? Most international organisations will have some preferred supplier agents who specialise in relocation services. Visits to such agents should be organised in advance of the due diligence to allow you and your spouse to get a sense of the locations you could potentially live. Australia is a mature country in the sense that it has hosted expatriate leaders for many decades. Real estate agents and relocation agents are very experienced in helping new arrivals find appropriate accommodation. There are many small services in Australia that specialise in relocations on a one-on-one basis and these are useful as a complementary service to the multinational offerings.

The mindset of the family arriving in Australia is particularly important. For an expatriate family on their first overseas assignment this may feel like an adventure which opens the opportunity to experience a lifestyle they would not in their home country. Australia offers a diverse range of living styles such as beachside living, inner city café living and high-end shopping-district style living. For other families, an expatriate assignment may feel more like an imposition and therefore finding accommodation that minimises any frustration is important. Time in different suburbs, sitting in coffee shops and getting a sense of what it would feel like to live there is time well spent. The ambitious executive who is finally getting the overseas posting they always wanted will have a natural desire to rush into the business to understand what they can do there. However, at this stage, family communication is a more important aspect to their skill set.

Selecting a school

There is no doubt that one of the biggest stresses for expatriate families is selecting the right school for their children. The quality of education in Australia is by international standards quite high, and there are a range of public and private schools from which to choose. As with any school choice the desires of the parents in terms of the outputs for the children will be reflected in the choice of school they feel is best for that child.

Another consideration is the accessibility to the school from home. This is often a significant influence on the choice of where to live or vice versa. Making appointments to visit a handful of schools is important, particularly for the spouse who will have the main responsibility for taking the children to school, or transporting them to their bus or train station, when in Australia.

Transport

Modern Australia is well equipped in terms of roads, buses, light rail and train systems. However, driving your own car is the most popular form of transport in Australia. It is not unusual for families to own and operate several cars.

Australians drive on the left-hand side of the road, which can be challenging at first if this is unfamiliar.

With the invention of GPS systems, hiring a car in a new city is no longer as daunting as it might have been. The ability to hire a car at the airport with a GPS makes exploration of a new city far easier. It is highly recommended that you drive yourself for at least part of the time on your visit. This not only gives an understanding of geography but also traffic patterns that would be encountered if the relocation takes place.

Rush hour in Sydney and Melbourne is typically up to two hours long whereas in Adelaide, Perth or Brisbane it can be as short as 30 minutes. Having a sense of what transport options are available from the suburb where you want to live and where the new office is located is a good insight to have before negotiating for the role.

Hanging out in the city

One of the comments most expatriate leaders make when they arrive in Australia is how much they enjoy the restaurant and café culture in the major cities. They are surprised at the level of sophistication and the quality of food they experience. Even though Australian cities are becoming expensive places to live, this is more than compensated for by the quality of food served in our eateries.

Taking time to relax and sit in coffee shops is a useful way to discuss with your spouse what has been found on the due diligence trip but also to learn insights into how life is lived in Australia.

Successful expatriate leaders are keen to observe the nuances of local life in a new city so they can use these insights later in one-on-one meetings and town hall meetings when they talk about what they have learnt about Australia since their arrival. Comments about the quality of the coffee in cafés, the type of food, the kind of books and newspapers people read are easy sources of material to use in later conversations. They also become interesting sources of excitement to tell the children back home once the decision to relocate has been made.

Negotiating the contract

Nine months after he started, Martin confessed to his coach he felt an ongoing sense of resentment to the organisation as he felt underpaid on this assignment. Because he was keen to get the position, he had accepted without negotiating. He subsequently found the cost of living in Australia far greater than he had bargained for and the cost of sending his two children to a private French school was putting a large dent in the weekly income. He admitted peers had advised him that he could negotiate before accepting the offer, as he was the preferred candidate. However, in the excitement and flattery of being offered the role he had neither negotiated nor done adequate due diligence. Nine months later the sense of resentment was now taking over his ability to perform as leader in a new country.

Like any kind of offer and acceptance, be it buying and selling houses, cars or executive positions in international organisations, negotiation plays an important part. Today, given the sophistication of organisations in terms of dealing with expatriate roles, most organisations have a very clear process with clear financial bands that are available to the executive. This does not mean, however, they are not negotiable or open to conversations about other points of interest to the executive. Some key areas that are worth exploring include the following.

The move itself
In most cases, transportation from your home country to Australia (including transporting furniture) is an automatic part of the process but it is worth clarifying the arrival dates of furniture to Australia. Given the distance, shipping times can vary depending on suppliers and having the family furniture arrive within a short period after the family arrives will accelerate a successful transition into a new country.

Flights
Flights to Australia are long! From Europe via Asia the average flight time is 22 hours. Negotiating business class flights for all the family means energy on arrival will be maximised.

Visits home
Many organisations offer one trip per year back to your home country, and some are open to second or third trips for your spouse and children. Given the leader is likely to travel to Europe or the United States for business meetings they are often able to organise trips back to their family as part of those business trips. However, for the spouse and children this is not the case. The ability to add in a second or third trip can make the initial transition more palatable.

Base salary

Base salary is always a point of contention and interest. Most organisations today have salary bands that are internationally based and moderated with bonuses based upon the local affiliate performance. Understanding the minimum and maximum range of the desired salary band is an important starting point with the negotiation. In Australia, the living away from home allowance (LAFHA) was disbanded in 2012. This has a net effect of reducing the take-home pay for expatriate leaders living in Australia. Understanding the percentage difference in net pay is important to allow you to negotiate with the organisation on achieving an equitable outcome.

Accommodation

Understanding the levels and duration of accommodation support is important. The preferred suburbs and housing styles will be made known on your due diligence visit and understanding in advance which parts of this are paid for by the organisation allows negotiations to take place. Having your family settle in a house they enjoy will accelerate your transition success.

Transport

Some organisations automatically include a company car with the position while some organisations do not. Understanding this in advance again allows negotiation to take place. Some expatriate leaders who choose to live near the company office opt to have a car for their spouse as opposed to themselves. Other expatriates choose to take the dollar value of the car as opposed to the car itself and therefore buy two smaller cars: one for them and one for their spouse. The options are endless as long as the leader knows in advance how the offer looks.

School fees

The Australian school system offers three levels of choices in terms of fees. There are public schools, systemic Catholic schools and private schools which includes international schools, religious denominations and non-denomination schools. Many expatriate families choose to send their children to private schools. Having the school fees included as part of the employment package becomes part of the negotiations.

Bonus structure

Most organisations structure the bonus for the organisational leader to reflect organisational performance (i.e. they will receive 30 per cent of their base salary presuming the organisation hits X and Y targets). The phase of growth of the business and the leadership mandate will have a large implication on what bonus structure and target structure should be accepted as part of the role. While this is not necessarily part of the negotiations with the job offer, it does become part of a negotiation process within the first six months of the role.

Managing the announcements

The phone rang. Susan picked it up. José, Vice President of International Operations was on the line. 'Congratulations, you are now the new GM of Australia,' he told her. 'I will have my EA draft an announcement to go out later on today.' Once Susan hung up from José she rang her current leader, Bill, to tell him. He suggested that from this point on she needed to manage her transitions and not just leave it up to the organisation. Based upon his experience, once a leader lets go of the process, including company announcements, they end up relenting control of their overall transition. 'Work with José and his people to ensure what he needs is achieved, but make sure you're in control of these activities,' he offered to Susan. 'By the way, congratulations on your new role,' he added. 'I'm going to miss you working for me.'

The announcement from the organisation is the first public sign a transition is happening. It lets the people in the new country know they have a new leader arriving. It allows the people who are currently reporting to the leader in the home country know their boss is departing and it signals a shift in operational leadership in its international affiliates.

While the generic wording of each announcement is similar and you will be able to finesse announcements at a local level, getting some key facts consistent is important. The first thing you need to do is negotiate your official pre-start and start dates. The pre-start date is a date you and your boss agree will be the date you actually start the role. This will involve one-on-one meetings, stakeholder meetings, business understanding meetings etc. The official start date is later so that expectations are not raised too early. Having an official start date about a month after the pre-start date allows you to settle your family in to the new home, to get familiar with key processes, school agendas, transport etc. and then to be able to hit the ground running on the official start date. Therefore, in any official announcements include a starting date this needs to be negotiated in advance.

Liaising with the local HR Director in Australia also allows them to pre-empt an international announcement and give the heads-up to the leadership team in Australia as well as key staff who may need to understand in advance of an international announcement. It also allows you to let your current team know you will be departing and an announcement is imminent. Some key points to include in an international message include:

- an announcement that you are taking the new role
- your new title
- the date you start the new role
- how excited you are at the new position
- your successes in their current role which explain your promotion
- congratulations and thank you to your predecessor.

At the home location, you can work with your team and HR business partner to craft a message for your current business. This will be similar to the international message but will highlight key activities that have been achieved at a local level under your leadership, your pride in the outputs of the organisation and your desire to wish them well.

Getting to know your new boss

One of the most important meetings in the pre-arrival phase is spending time with your new boss. Inevitably, when someone is leaving a functional role and moving to a general management role, particularly if for the first time, their new boss will be keen to ensure the mandate for the job is clearly understood. Understanding the expectations of the role and of the leader in the new expatriate assignment is key to hitting the ground running.

Some key areas to cover in this initial meeting follow:

Clarity of expectations of the role
- Where does this role fit in the overall organisational structure and how important is it in delivering the business strategy?
- What is the overall business strategy and therefore the accompanying mandate?
- Is the organisation comfortable with the strategy or does it need reworking?
- What are the assumed targets and goals stemming from this strategy?
- What are the budgets the organisation is working on and what is the state of the revenue?

- Where are the mismatches between targets, budgets and realities?
- How do expectations compare with the current performance levels (i.e. is there a performance gap)?
- If there is a performance gap, what is the leap in performance needed and what are the underlying reasons?

Clarity around the organisational culture

- From the viewpoint of an international leader, how are things done in the Australian affiliate and to what degree are they done well?
- How are decisions made, both formally and informally?
- What kind of behaviour is valued?
- How bureaucratic or casual is the Australian affiliate?
- What is the pace of change and the acceptance of that?
- What are the espoused values?
- Are the values merely 'written on the wall' or 'walked in the hall' (i.e. are they lived)?

Leadership team

- What are the strengths and weaknesses of the Australian leadership team?
- From an international perspective, how well do they operate as a team?
- From an international perspective, how are they perceived across the wider organisation?
- How are they perceived by their suppliers/vendors?
- Is there anybody at the local level who is expected to get the GM or MD role? If so, is there any potential for resentment lurking in the Australian affiliate?
- How many members of the Australian leadership team are on a talent map for future development?

The nature of the peer group

- What does the international leader expect of his/her direct reports as a peer group?
- What are the peers' and individuals' strengths and weaknesses?
- Do they operate as a team or as a functional reporting working group?
- Who are the natural leaders amongst the peer group?
- Who are the natural influencers amongst the peer group?
- What are the expectations the leader has of the Australian GM as part of the peer group?
- What are the normal meeting arrangements — face-to-face or telephone conference?

Management style of your new boss

- What are the priorities and pressures?
- How do they like to communicate and be communicated with?
- What kind of relationship do they like to have with direct reports/your peers?
- What are the regular one-on-one meetings they would like to have?
- What are the preferred formal and informal communication channels?
- How often do they like to come to Australia to do business review meetings?

When Brendan took on the new role as Head of Australia for a nutrition business, he also inherited a new boss. This is quite common for most expatriate leaders when they take on a new assignment. Learning to work with your boss in the first couple of weeks is an essential accelerator to success. Unfortunately, Brendan did not take the time to learn how to work with his new boss.

Brendan had previously worked with someone who was charismatic, who did not manage details and who took a close interest in Brendan personally. On the other hand, his new boss, Sharma, had a PhD in mathematics and came from a financial auditing background. He was keenly interested in the detail of almost every spreadsheet Brendan developed. Six months later, when Brendan was struggling to work with Sharma and getting increasingly frustrated at what he thought was micro-management, his coach reminded Brendan that it was his duty to change his style to suit Sharma and not necessarily Sharma's duty to change his style to suit Brendan.

Once Brendan realised he had not spent time in understanding how best to work with Sharma and indeed that Sharma's style was quite different to that of his previous boss, he realised he had to 'start again'. He sought a meeting with Sharma and explained he had not taken the time to understand Sharma's preferences and would almost like to start afresh. Sharma explained the reason behind his desire for detail and that it was not coming from a micro-management perspective but that up the line he was being pressured for detail. Sharma said he'd learnt over the years that once he fully understood a business and how it operated, he was then able to back off from understanding the details.

With that in mind, Brendan and his team worked to develop a scorecard system with agreed metrics between him and Sharma. As a result, Sharma had less need for detailed spreadsheets and uses the balanced scorecard as a mechanism to moderate his questions.

Brendan also practically readjusted the agenda for his one-on-one meetings with Sharma to allow for more conversations on the business metrics upfront and questions about people later.

A year later, Brendan confessed that having changed his style, albeit six months too late, he actually learnt a lot about the financial management of the business by working with Sharma and was quite grateful for having the opportunity of working with him.

Getting your mandate

Chris came to Australia as the new Country Head, having previously done a three-year role as the Head of the South Korean business. Originally from Texas, Chris was a bright, intelligent man who believed in his own capabilities.

He had been sent to South Korea to get experience in a very different culture and this was his first experience in a GM role. The South Korean business was considered quite small but geographically and culturally close to Japan, which was a major market for the organisation. Chris was successful in South Korea and was promoted to lead the Australian business.

For a variety of reasons, Chris did not have (nor did he create) the opportunity to sit down with his boss to fully understand the Australian business, the organisational needs of that business and the mandate of the new role. He said that he previously had experience as a GM and, having worked in the broader Asia area, was quite comfortable he could quickly pick up the business in Australia. In his first three months, his boss was also promoted and therefore it took at least another three months before Chris had a proper sit-down with his new boss. By this point, he had driven a change process he considered to be important, despite resistance from the local leadership team.

Chris underestimated the communication channels that existed between Australia and head office. He also largely ignored the muttering and taunts being made to him about his change process. At the six-month mark, when he finally got to sit down with his new boss, Chris got a stern warning that he was leading the business ineffectively as he had never taken time to understand what the business really needed. He was told that leading in South Korea is considered to be the first step for a baby GM. While he had not made any large mistakes, he didn't lead brilliantly there and the organisation was watching his performance in Australia to determine whether he would have a future international career.

Chris was shocked, and in discussions with his coach he realised the mistake he made was not getting a clear mandate from the international organisation as to what was needed in the Australian affiliate. His assumptions were based upon incorrect information and lack of detailed knowledge. Chris left the organisation four months later.

What Chris failed to do was to accurately match the strategy to the business situation. According to a range of organisational writers and scholars there are normally five different phases a business can be in: start-up, sustain and grow, realign, turnaround and shut-down. What tends to happen is that business cycles back and forth between these phases. The phase the business is currently in will help determine what the international organisation wants of the business, the leadership mandate and how they should go about leading at the local level.

We'll now take a look at those five phases in detail.

Start-up

In the start-up phase a leader's mandate is to ignite the organisation. You are asked to put together the broad capability such as people, investment funds, technology platforms, vendor and supplier relationships, and to find the initial customers. In an international organisation, start-up is usually when an organisation decides to enter a new geographical territory for the first time or decides to launch a new product or service. The leader needs to have lots of energy because the success rate for start-ups is low, and if operating in a new geographical territory both the leader and the organisation are often learning for the first time how to operate in that new country.

Sustain and grow

In the sustain and grow phase the leader is responsible for nourishing the organisation to build it from one level to the next. This is a phase of enjoyable leadership in the sense that you get to seek out and invent new challenges and bring the organisation along a pathway not previously explored. Often the leader can take their time in doing this, depending on the external market forces and cash flow opportunities. The leader in this environment spends time learning and developing organisational culture and political systems, and needs to be adept at building supporting coalitions.

Realign

In the realign phase the leader's role is to reposition the business away from or distinctly towards a new way of operating. Usually the organisation is drifting into trouble, has lost its focus, has dropped its sense of accountability or has fallen into complacency. While this phase is not a true change phase in the sense of a turnaround, the leader does need to embody a sense of urgency, pace setting, clarity of vision and momentum to reinvigorate a business unit or organisation.

Turnaround

The turnaround phase is when the leader needs to engage a major shift in the organisation. Typically the organisation is in financial trouble or the projections suggest it will be. Disruptive changes to the industry by competitors may have forced the organisation's hand, or any lack of success in the realign phase may suggest a stronger change management program is needed. In this phase a leader needs courage and strength of will, to be adept at actively shifting the culture and shifting the mindset of the leadership team. The phrase 'change the people or change the people' is an active mantra for leaders who actively engage in major shifts of organisations.

Shut-down

Finally, the shut-down phase occurs when an organisation decides an affiliate is no longer viable or no longer part of its long-term strategy, or has decided to offshore particular services that used to be provided at a local level. In this phase a leader needs to engage with humanity to honour and respect the employees who have served the organisation, and to deal with government and external vendor relationships that have been part of their legacy. Successful leaders in this phase take a leadership view of acknowledging that life happens in ways we often least expect and try to serve the interests of the people being affected as well as the needs of the organisation.

Having a clear mandate from the organisation and understanding the business phase where the affiliate finds itself are starting points for you as the new expatriate leader. This needs to be done before you arrive in the country, which will allow mental preparation in terms of personal psychology and energy levels needed. It also allows a self-assessment of your capabilities and preferences in leadership style before you arrive.

Self-assessment against the task

The final stage in the pre-arrival phase is seeking feedback from current peers, current direct reports and your most recent boss, to understand your strengths and weaknesses so as to form an honest view about how you match up against the mandate and role requirements.

Quite often, expatriate leaders receive feedback a year or two after they have started their assignment, which resonates with feedback they had received three years earlier but neglected to acknowledge. Leadership derailers are part of every leader's psyche but on a bigger stage they become amplified. The great thing, however, is that the positive things also become amplified on a bigger stage.

Given the number of transitions you will be going through in an expatriate assignment, your natural derailers will peak during times of stress. Successful expatriate leaders are those who understand their own strengths and weaknesses. They develop the ability to regulate their behaviours and surround themselves with people who balance them.

Marshall Goldsmith, whose organisation I work closely with in Australia, is considered to be one of the most influential international leadership writers. Marshall has been regularly placed as the most influential coach in the world and is rated in the top ten on the Leadership Guru list. In his book, *What Got You Here Won't Get You There*, Goldsmith noted that asking for 'feed forward' is a useful strategy to accelerate behaviour change and leadership adaptability.[3] His view that involving stakeholders in a proactive manner has been proven to be a key factor in long-term successful behaviour change at a leadership level. Many international coaches have since adopted this strategy, including our own firm. From an expat executive perspective the idea is to identify fellow leaders such as peers, direct reports and one-up or two-up leaders, who have observed you at close quarters over the preceding years, and ask the following questions:

- I am going overseas on assignment; do you have any suggestions for what I should focus on given how well you know me?
- Based on the answer to the above question, do you have any specific behavioural tips for me in terms of what I should/should not do?

Pre-arrival checklist

- Negotiate a package that best serves the organisation, the role and you and your family before you leave for Australia.

- Actively involve your spouse in a pre-arrival visit to Australia and ensure s/he is involved in the accommodation, school and transport choices.
- Coordinate the various announcement messages at a local and international level.
- Negotiate a pre-starting date and an official starting date and have up to a month between the two dates.
- Spend time with your new boss to understand their leadership preferences and operating styles.
- Learn about your new peers and the various operating rhythms that exist for both face-to-face and virtual meetings.
- Seek out a clear mandate in terms of what the organisation needs of you in this new role.
- Assess the business for what phase it is actually in and whether it needs to move to a different phase.
- Assess your strengths and weaknesses against this mandate. Seek feedback and 'feed forward' from those who know you well and put in place a plan to address any gaps that exist.
- Create a learning agenda before arriving in Australia that reflects both your learning preferences and any gaps identified above.

7

THE ARRIVAL PHASE

Skills needed

At an individual level, self-management is needed to balance the mixed emotions of starting a new role in a strange environment overseas, knowing that everyone is watching your moves to understand who you are as a leader.

At an organisational level, delivering clear and prepared messages to individuals and groups upon your arrival will set the scene for your first few weeks.

Key question

What is the initial impact I need to have?

Key outcome

A clear presentation to the organisation.

'Ladies and gentlemen, boys and girls, please fasten your seatbelts, we are about to begin our descent into Sydney ...'. Joe looked across at Susan. 'We're about to begin our big adventure,' he said. They had left Chicago three days earlier, having a stop-off in Hong Kong, and were now arriving in Sydney for what they hoped would be a successful and enjoyable expatriate asssignment.

Having done some online research pre-arrival they were somewhat familiar with the immigration procedures and had liaised with the migration agent appointed by the organisation. Their first surprise came at the customs barrier. They were not aware that Australia has the strictest quarantine controls in the world. Cory, aged fifteen, was asked to leave his bag of lychees in the fruit bin at the quarantine area after they had been detected by sniffer dogs. He had never come across such exotic Asian fruits before and had brought a bag with him from Hong Kong, not realising he would be unable to bring them into Australia.

Susan's company had organised for a car and driver to pick them up at the airport and take them to their city-based hotel, where they would spend their first week. Zach, aged fourteen, had already taken over 300 photographs on his iPhone and uploaded them to his Facebook page before they had even got into the car!

For most people the initial arrival to their new country is filled with excitement. They have done some preliminary research and, usually, the accommodation and initial transport arrangements have been made in advance. Most families stay in a city-based hotel for anywhere from a week to a couple of months while their more permanent accommodation is organised. This gives a sense of holiday and accentuates the honeymoon period most people feel.

Ideally, you and your family will have arrived a few days in advance of your pre-start date and will therefore be able to explore the city together. Taking time to explore the sights of the city, even if it means doing the standard bus tour every tourist does, is encouraged. Particularly for families with teenage children, having a sense of the city gives them a feeling of wonder and expectation for when they will explore solo or with new mates after they settle in. Doing these things gives an overall sense of where they will live in relation to the city and lands the concept of 'we are now starting a new life somewhere else'.

The pre-start

Susan took advice from her former boss and negotiated a pre-start and an official start date with a two-week difference. This allowed her time to settle in her family and also to meet with key stakeholders and direct reports to develop an understanding of the organisation before her official start date. The real estate organisation, with whom they had liaised, secured them accommodation in the suburb of Mosman, on the northern side of Sydney. They were due to move into the apartment four days after arrival. They also organised rental furniture for up to six weeks thus allowing them to move into a fully furnished apartment immediately. Having negotiated a faster shipping option, their own furniture was due to arrive within a month.

Susan and Joe deliberately decided to spend the first three days exploring the city with their children and then took two days to move into the new apartment. Susan felt very comfortable knowing that within the first week the family would be housed, settled and starting to create their own routine.

On her second day she woke up early and decided to take a walk around the botanic gardens to think through the various transition hurdles she knew she would possibly encounter.

Planning to overcome transition hurdles

As discussed earlier, every expatriate (and indeed every new leader) experiences various transitions. In total there are seven major hurdles the expat leader needs to overcome. It is first important to acknowledge that there will be hurdles and then to have a plan to address them.

The seven transition hurdles are as follows.

Fully understanding the organisation

Many expatriate leaders accept assignments in overseas roles without fully understanding the 'state' of the organisation for which they are bound. The excitement of their first overseas assignment dwarfs the necessity to understand what the role will require of them.

For a variety of reasons they may inherit an organisation that lacks clarity, may be in a phase of decline or has previously had a dysfunctional leader or leadership team that has left the organisation lacking overall direction.

Understanding the real and current state of the organisation and getting a clear mandate from the region's international leader is an essential tactic for the new leader. If this has not been done in the pre-arrival phase it needs to be done very quickly upon arrival. Not seeking a clear mandate or not venturing to ask the tough questions will inevitably lead to an unclear picture or, worse, a faulty understanding and sense of security as to what to expect when arriving in the new country.

Fully understanding the role

A lack of clarity, expectations and understanding of the role's structure and its positioning relative to the rest of the organisation often leads to disappointment.

The nature of multinational organisations is that they are often a range of matrix structures existing in affiliate regions away from head office. This can lead to a situation where the country head finds their direct reports have a hard line to offshore leaders but only a dotted line to them. By nature this means the country head's overall authority and governance ability is limited.

George, a very experienced sales leader in the United States, found himself as a new expatriate in Australia with what he considered a very strong remuneration package obtained through his excellent negotiation ability. However, when he commenced his role in Melbourne he discovered that three of the seven direct reports were only dotted line reports to him and each had their main reporting line to different leaders offshore. His ability to enforce a strategic change process was thwarted by the needs of the other leaders in a matrix structure. He soon realised that his negotiation ability, while useful, was limited in setting him up for real success in the role.

Fully understanding stakeholders' needs

Every organisation has a range of stakeholders. Internal stakeholders can be found both within the physical organisation at a local level and across the wider organisation internationally. External stakeholders can include customers, collaborative partners, research organisations, vendors and government agencies. Many executives fail to recognise and map out their stakeholders and assess each stakeholder's importance in helping achieve the overall mandate. There are countless examples of executives realising six to twelve months after their arrival that some of their efforts have been sabotaged, purposefully or not, by someone who feels aggrieved that the leader had not taken time to meet with them or understand their needs. As a result, the stakeholder felt they had been deemed unimportant and did not take kindly to the perceived insult. (Read more about this in Chapter 8.)

Liam was surprised when his coach recommended he take a few days to meet with stakeholders prior to his official start date. Liam instinctively felt he needed to meet everybody internally before he ventured outside the door. He was reminded that one of his key mandates was to reverse the perception of poor customer centricity in the Australian affiliate and therefore spending time with the customers would help him understand why this perception actually existed.

Coming from Ireland, Liam had a natural ability in conversation and later he expressed his affinity with Australian culture. He found that by conducting a range of stakeholder interviews he picked up patterns allowing him to understand why the perception of poor customer centricity existed.

When he officially started and had his first town hall meeting where he addressed the organisation, he was able to eloquently and credibly articulate the issues the organisation faced using examples from the three most important customer groups. He said later that in his first week, two of the most successful sales representatives came to see him. They expressed gratitude he had taken time to meet with customer groups and expressed their relief that at last someone was addressing the core issues they face every single day in the market-place. Liam laughingly retold these stories later as the two Australian sales representatives had said to him, 'We thought having come from Ireland you would not understand our market but boy were we wrong — you understand it more than some of the people who have worked here all their lives.'

Fully listening to the 'saids and unsaids'

The typical mistake leaders in transition, particularly expatriate leaders, make is not taking enough time to fully understand the history of the organisation, how it works, the culture, how decisions get made and how the current strategy was developed. Not making time to understand the key influences across the organisation such as customers, capability and market conditions will eventually trip you up.

A natural response for new leaders is to aim for speed to show they can execute, which often overlooks the need to fully understand what actually must be executed. The ability to systemically meet with a range of stake-holders inside and outside the organisation, to ask deep and penetrating questions and to take the time to reflect and understand the organisation and local country culture are skills that most leaders have to develop or at least build upon. Socrates said 'Wisdom begins in wonder'. The most successful expatriate leaders have a 'curious' mindset and want to learn about the organisation and what makes it tick. (More about this phase can be found in Chapter 8.)

Fully leading the leadership team

Unless the organisation is in a start-up phase, all expatriate leaders will inherit a leadership team that existed before their arrival. Taking time to understand each individual, their capability and how the overall team works is an important part of leadership. Without an effective leader-ship team, the organisation cannot be effective. Organisational culture is hugely influenced by the culture created by and amongst the leadership team in how they work together. Studies from international organisations such as Human Synergistics and Gallup suggest organisational culture is influenced up to 80 per cent by the impact of the leadership team.

Irrespective of how successful a team was previously, it will always start again when a new leader arrives. The team will slow down to the level of the new leader and wait for the leader to take charge and help set a new direction. Therefore, the leader needs to follow a process, at the outset conduct a 'new leader assimilation' exercise and then move on to use the '5Q process' (both outlined in later chapters) to help guide the team towards high performance.

Fully leading oneself

There has never been and never will be a perfect leader. By the mere fact we are human beings means we bring strengths, weaknesses and blind spots to work every single day. The larger the blind spot and weakness, the lower the level of self-awareness and, therefore, the lower the level of self-regulation. This applies to every leader at every level.

Even the most successful leaders will admit they have made and continue to make many mistakes. John Mackey, CEO of Whole Foods in the United States, says that with the benefit of hindsight he can recognise that Whole Foods stalled and slowed every time his leadership plateaued. 'It always took someone else to help me increase my awareness and change the way I was leading for the organisation to grow'.[1]

As outlined in the previous chapter, in the pre-arrival phase we recommend you conduct an assessment of yourself through conversations with your peers and direct reports, so as to have a very frank understanding of your strengths and gaps. You need to understand that whatever gaps or weaknesses you have will be amplified in a new and strange environment. Admitting one has gaps or weaknesses is a sign of vulnerability and honesty — both traits of potentially great leadership.

Fully developing adaptability

The pace of change in the business world has never been faster. The worldwide web was born in 1989 and transformed the way we connect. Google was born in 1998 and has transformed the way we get and manage our information. It is estimated that just one daily edition of the *Sydney Morning Herald* contains more information than someone living in the eighteenth century received in their entire lifetime. At high school level, it is estimated that of the curriculum students learn today, almost one-third will be changed by the time they graduate.

The implication of all this change is that the best laid plans may not be executed or even realised a year or two after being set. Planning and managing are important. However, the observation of the output and impacts and tailoring towards those is even more important.

Go online at www.foreignerincharge.com for a copy of a checklist and downloadable action-planning sheet to overcome the transition hurdles.

When Alex arrived from California to take up a senior role in one of Australia's telecommunication organisations he was quite clear about the nature of the turnaround needed. He had been given a crystal clear mandate from the CEO who hired him. However, six months later Alex openly admitted the degree of change needed was far greater than anyone expected and the plans developed four months earlier were not the plans now needed to execute the change. Having had no issue with admitting mistakes or under-standing that change happens rapidly, particularly in his industry, Alex reoriented his team to a different mandate and adapted very quickly. The learning at an organisation level was that change was the new 'business as usual', and therefore constant monitoring, evaluation and adaptation were the key skills needed to lead towards turnaround.

In a public forum to the organisation Alex outlined the original plans and why they no longer made sense. In an attempt to explain the rapid nature of change he asked the audience to remember who they were as people five years ago, then one year ago and then last month. In doing so he explained that in hindsight change happens continually and that as human beings we rarely stay still for very long. In fact, we look back on our lives and wonder how we used to be that person that we know we used to be!

While some people in the organisation were confused and uncomfortable with the relentlessness and unpredictability of the change, most employees accepted that this was the best way forward. Alex's approach of using the personal change metaphor went down really well and became a water-cooler conversation topic for weeks. Many people were heard discussing who they used to be and how glad they were to no longer be that person.

The first day

Your first day and first few days in the new role are very exciting. They are also very important in that the organisation is watching their new leader. The concept of the 'shadow of the leader' is an important one for every expatriate leader to understand and appreciate. The shadow of a leader is the wake, influence or impact they leave behind them. Imagine you are in a meeting and you walk out of the room — what is said about you after you've left is the shadow you have cast across that meeting. The more senior a leader is, the larger the shadow they cast.

The shadow may not be visible to you as it may lie behind you. Unless you are actively seeking to understand the shadow (in the case of leadership this means seeking feedback on a regular basis), most leaders are unaware of the shadow they cast. However, taking a proactive management approach to your leadership shadow can serve to minimise unintentional mistakes.

In conjunction with a local Human Resources Director, successful expatriate leaders tend to have a predefined agenda on their first day. Although there is no set or mandated agenda, typically it can look like this:

- Breakfast with the HR Director or the members of the leadership team.
- A walk around the building for a meet and greet with key staff in their various functions.
- A company-wide (town hall) morning tea or lunch where the leader is welcomed and potentially gives a short address to the organisation.
- A one-on-one meeting with their Executive Assistant to understand diary protocols, communication preferences and what is already in the diary over the next week or two.
- One-on-one meetings with direct reports as a follow-up to a request for their business plans to have a top-line understanding of where each function is performing.
- Request to sit in on each functional meeting (i.e. sit in on the financial team's meeting, the sales team's meeting, the marketing team's meeting etc).
- Attend any mandatory on-boarding sessions to the organisation. These typically are shortened and accelerated for the new leader to ensure they get across all vital information as quickly as possible.
- And finally, at the end of the day a drinks meet and greet in an informal setting.

There are many variations of this agenda and they will all depend upon the organisation and the situation, but being prepared for the first day underlines the impression the leader is trying to create.

Colin arrived in Australia from London, having previously worked in Japan and the United States. He knew in advance that the business needed to enter a very urgent turnaround phase and that morale amongst staff was probably low. The reputation of the organisation had been battered in the public media and had even been written about in the international press. Colin's arrival in Australia was signalled in the financial press as having been to 'save the company'.

Knowing that the broader organisation would be watching him very acutely given the state of the business, Colin opted to spend the second half of his first day walking around the building to meet staff.

He spoke to almost everyone in the building either one-on-one or in small groups, albeit for short periods of time. However, the feedback from staff at the end of his first week was glowing. The Human Resources Director later recalled, 'There is nothing I would have asked him to do differently in his first week. I can tangibly feel a difference in our morale by the mere fact he has gone and spoken to everybody. His ability to listen to stories and understand people's concerns has made a palpable difference to the business already.'

An Australian supermarket chain that went through a phase of bringing in executives from the United Kingdom for senior roles realised the impression made by the expat executives on the first day and week was inherently important for their future success in Australia. As part of the preparation for their first town hall meeting, held in Melbourne, the organisation encouraged each executive to identify a local football club (AFL) to support. Melbourne is obsessed with Australian Football League, more commonly known as Aussie Rules. When talking to someone in or from Melbourne it is helpful to know which team they support and to be able to have a basic conversation about the competition. Having a new boss who already supports a team creates an initial shared interest and signals 'this person is part of our culture even if they support a rival team'.

8

THE LOOK, LISTEN AND LEARN PHASE

Skills needed

At an individual level, the key skill is listening deeply to all the 'saids and unsaids' to understand the local landscape. This helps in gaining perspective.

At a leadership team level, the skill is to observe the team, how it operates and currently leads the organisation.

Key question

What do I need to fully understand in order to lead this business?

Key outcome

Perspective.

Susan could hear Bill's voice in her head: 'Don't forget — seek first to understand ...' She had been in her new organisation for ten days and the family was starting to settle down in their new life in Sydney. Susan was taking the next couple of weeks to understand the business, to build a perspective of where it was and where it needed to be based upon the mandate José had given her.

Her pre-assessment analysis of her own skill set had told her that her natural bias for action would mean she would want to jump in to solving any issues immediately. The 'feed forward' she had received was to listen well and resist the temptation to jump into fix-it mode until she really understood the context and issues. She reminded herself she had to take the time to fully understand the issues before acting, as this would risk making assumptions that may prove to be invalid.

One of the nuances of leading in Australia as an expat is the view the followers hold of the leader. While Australia looks and often feels like countries such as the United Kingdom and the United States, it holds a different perspective about leaders.

Australians respect the role of leadership and leaders but this does not automatically translate into respect for the person in the leadership role. It may feel to the new leader like the Australian team member is standing with arms folded across their chest, thinking 'Go on! Prove to me how good you really are!' This is probably because this is actually what is happening.

Australians can take the view that just because someone has been put into the role of leader this does not necessarily mean they have great leadership qualities. This may be accentuated if a team member feels they should have been appointed to the position. They are now watching the new leader to see what qualities this person has that they don't. There is a strong belief in meritocracy in Australian society and therefore leaders are expected to earn their right to lead.

This does not mean the Australian leadership team will actively try to sabotage the new leader. On the contrary, they will work to help the new leader. However, they tend to meet the leader only halfway with the expectation that the leader will also make an effort to meet them at that point. This means the new expatriate leader needs to work hard to prove themself in the first couple of weeks and months.

Many expatriate leaders have fallen into the trap of assuming that because they were successful elsewhere they will automatically be successful in their new role in Australia. Also, their experience may have been that a leader's positional power commands and receives automatic respect and followership. This is not the case in Australia. So taking the time to be purposeful and planned will enhance the likelihood of success.

In the pressure of taking on a new role there is a desire to execute and be seen to act. This can result in the rush to act without considering all the necessary dynamics and may create a suboptimal longer-term outcome.

Thanks to Michael Watkins and other writers, we are well aware of the importance of setting up a plan to assist in a successful first three months. Our experience is that many people understand the importance of creating a plan but often don't identify the key areas for which to plan, focusing on one or two areas rather than taking a holistic approach.

Managing your learning process

A great first quarter plan can only be developed based on good data obtained through accessing the right sources, probing for the right information and then assimilating this in a useful and practical way to inform action. The necessary first step is to have a robust learning process in place. A learning process is divided into two distinctly different areas: effective learning and efficient learning.

Effective learning involves deciding what you need to learn so as to focus the right perspectives and make the right decisions for the organisation as quickly as possible.

Efficient learning involves identifying the best sources for learning, insight and knowledge and how to do so in the shortest time possible.[1] Sources of insight spread across and outside of the organisation. Structured learning can be both formal and informal and occurs both within and outside of the organisation.

Applying perspective

Once you have information and insight, the next step is to take action. Every leader needs to develop and act upon perspectives. Perspectives can come from many sources and angles. The more senior a leader is, the more tacit (that is, work-related practical know-how learnt on the job) their accumulated knowledge.

Researchers suggest tacit knowledge exists on the fringe of awareness, probably just outside consciousness. It is a powerful source of knowledge for strategic development as executives are able to back-translate their stored knowledge and relate it to the issues being faced in the current role. However, researchers also say tacit knowledge is developed over time and through a broad questioning approach.

Tony Grant, the well-known Australian coaching academic and author of *Coach Yourself* says great leaders, who develop a coaching style of leadership, also develop a strong ability to recognise patterns.[2] Matt Church, co-author of *Thought Leaders*, says perspective is about seeing patterns in everything going on around you.[3]

There are six major abilities leaders can use to develop their perspective.

Look and listen

For a Westerner arriving in a country such as Mongolia it is relatively easy to notice what is different. The language is different, the tonality sounds harsh, and people's habits are unfamiliar.

It is easy to identify patterns that are different in an organisation or country which is in stark contrast to the one from which you came. However, for most expats Australia will appear familiar on many fronts. English is spoken, many habits seem European or American, the food is international and there's a universal culture around sport.

You will have to make a more active effort to listen to words, narratives and phrases to understand the underlying meaning. Observing people in meetings or wherever they congregate, watching the habits they exhibit, gives a sense of the organisational culture. Observing the formality or informality that takes place in external meetings gives a sense of how business is done in Australia. Notice what sporting codes are discussed in what kind of meetings. For example, notice that conversations about rugby league in Sydney are very different to the conversations about AFL in Melbourne.

Regular reflection

The ability to reflect is the key accelerator to building one's awareness. Understanding what is happening and making sense of that event relative to similar events you have previously experienced is the underlying skill to build perspective.

Observing new ways of working in a new country without judgement can open the possibility of new ways of doing things. Likewise, observing what practices seem substandard without any judgement allows you to approach people with a degree of empathy and curiosity.

Consider

It is easy to come into an organisation and spot all the gaps, observe the inadequacies and gain clarity on all the opportunities with a degree of arrogance and self-righteousness. Many leaders have made this mistake! However, the ability to step back and consider through the eyes of the people in the organisation why they have arrived in such a place is very useful. Doing the same through the eyes of other leaders is also very useful. Asking yourself 'What would Google or Apple do in this situation?' is a great way to build a sense of creativity.

Global analysis

One of the key benefits of organisations sending executives all over the world can be likened to a bee spreading pollen from one flower to another. One of the purposes of having executive leaders in different countries is to bring global perspectives to the local affiliate. The ability to take a local situation and look for similar issues or patterns in a global context gives you a broader perspective.

Root cause analysis

Taking time to do root cause analysis is an important facet in building perspective. While there may be similar issues in many different countries, there could be different causes at play locally. While global in some respects, the pharmaceutical industry, for example, has very different regulations in different countries.

At a personal level, a new leader also needs to understand their own reactions to information, events and incidents, especially if they tend to react in a somewhat negative manner. They need to understand their own **root cause analysis** (i.e. where they have acted like that before or what may be a catalyst for their current behaviour). Leadership scholars, such as Bob Anderson from The Leadership Circle, suggest a leader's reactionary behaviours are rooted in events and learning from earlier in their life that they have not yet overcome.[4] Therefore, noticing and understanding one's own reactions to events can help develop wider perspectives about the new local environment without getting trapped into regular assumptions based upon one's own history rather than the current reality. For example, if your parents were very perfectionistic in nature and you also learnt to lead in a micro-managing manner, you might react to the so-called relaxed nature of some Australian businesses with harsh judgement rather than looking beyond the obvious.

Reconsider

A business school researched the differences between the most successful leaders and their counterparts. The surprising outcome was the most successful leaders practised regular meditation or reflection. This allowed them to sharpen their intellectual ability by broadening their tacit knowledge and intuition. The skill of reconsidering and re-evaluating major decisions, the preceding root cause analysis, actions taken and their impacts, has a long-term growth effect on building perspective.

A first quarter plan

There is no right way to create a first quarter plan. Every organisation will have some unique nuances that will influence where to focus. However, there are several important key focus areas to consider when drafting up the plan. These include:

- managing self
- the organisational mandate and financials
- working with your boss and peers
- understanding your markets and customers
- understanding your current leadership team

- understanding the organisational culture
- how to get started
- how to keep building the family foundations.

We'll look at each of these, including outputs, questions and actions to be considered.

Managing self

You never get a second chance to make a first impression. Considering and planning how to project and manage yourself within the new dynamic can support the achievement of your leadership goals.

When talking with clients commencing new roles, we ask them 'How do you want to be thought of in the organisation?' The most common response is 'to be seen as credible and respected'. In spite of this, what we also find is that many executives actually sabotage, or at least make it extremely difficult for themselves to achieve this outcome.

Outputs

- Strong symbols and messaging about who you are and your expectations.
- Start out as you expect to continue.

Questions

- Do you have a conscious understanding of the impact you want to have on others?
- What is it you want people to be saying about you and your leadership after they have met you?
- How can you 'be' (behave, speak) in every interaction in order to promote this image?

Actions

- Pay attention to personal habits — every move you make will be subject to discussion and interpretation. Dress appropriately, turn up, be on time, be present (restrict personal organisation and logistics to set times and days).
- Talk with people — have conversations and build connections. Only share appropriate content and personal information.
- Be honest. The modern world is a small place. Being ambiguous or flexible with the truth about your history inevitably shows. Facebook and LinkedIn have revealed far too often the real history of a leader's story. Likewise, a leader giving a false reason or pretence for a new strategy inevitably gets found out. Australians like truth and candour, even if it is not always a good news story.

- Consider how you relate to people, allocate time, prepare for meetings.
- Find information 'interesting' without passing judgement.
- Contain your commentary about predecessors. There can be a conscious or unconscious tendency (arising from competitiveness) to discredit a predecessor. Even if there is a clear mandate that the business is in turnaround mode, it is gracious and respectful to give credit to the organisation's and leadership team's previous achievements. 'Blaming' or discrediting the previous leader only makes you look petty and makes people wonder how you will talk about them.
- Contain comparisons and commentary about how things were at your previous organisation.
- It may be too early for specific details about plans but you need to communicate the basic values that will serve as the framework for future decision making.
- Leaders need to set clear goals. This needs to happen within four to twelve weeks after arrival. The organisation naturally slows down to the pace of the leader and the leadership team. If the leader does not commit to goals, the organisation eventually slows to a halt, develops confusion or even chaos.
- Be clear about your style. How will you treat people and how should they treat you?

Trust

The concept of trust in organisations is not new. In his book *The Five Dysfunctions of a Team*, Patrick Lencioni suggests trust is the most important building block to a high-performing organisation or leadership team.[5] Surveys by the Gallup organisation in the last five years suggest trust in organisations has decreased since 2009 and had flat-lined by 2012.[6] The Edelman Trust Barometer has looked at similar sets of questionnaires and their findings are in agreement.

Studies show productivity, income and profits of organisations are positively or negatively impacted depending on the organisation's trust in its leader. A survey by Maritz suggested only 7 per cent of workers strongly agree they trusted senior leaders to look after their best interests.[7] The challenge for the new leader is to go about their business learning about the organisation and its issues and potential solutions while concurrently displaying the building blocks of trustworthiness.

The four elements leaders need to display that will build trust when connecting with the organisation for the first time are ability, believability, connectivity to their audience and dependability.

Ability is about demonstrating competence. In the 'look, listen and learn' phase you are seeking to understand the organisation and in doing so you demonstrate your past experience and potential competence. The way you ask questions, cipher information, clarify core issues and interact with a broad range of people gives an insight into your level of competency. Within the first 30 minutes of meeting you, employees will decide whether you are a leader worth following.

Believability. Australians are practical people. The geographical isolation of the country and the history of European settlement mean pragmatism usually reigns. The underbelly of pragmatism is what is referred to as a BS (or bullshit) detector! Australians size up leaders very quickly based upon whether they think their commentary is believable and whether their processes are equitable, consistent and sustainable.

Connectivity is about demonstrating genuine interest in other people. Leaders who are genuinely interested in the organisation, its history and issues of the prevailing market can demonstrate this through the questions they ask. The ability to be relatively open, share information about the organisation, themselves and the real side to their personality is always a bonus. Taking time to 'walk the floor' is very difficult for some leaders, particularly those who are introverted or who have come from technical roles. However, developing this ability is essential to developing the element of connectivity.

Dependability involves demonstrating the ability to consistently follow-through. Seeking to understand the issues and asking for feedback about potential solutions is a great first step. This needs to be followed up with visible and helpful actions. Australians tend to quickly lose faith in leaders if they do not do what they say they will do. This, of course, is no different to most countries.

Building trust in the early days of a new role is essential for an expat leader. Over our years of working with new leaders in Australia we've observed many mistakes, made intentionally or unintentionally, that have eroded trustworthiness. It would almost appear they have actively destroyed their own reputation!

When Leonard arrived in Sydney from San Francisco he was shocked at the organisational culture that awaited him. Even though he had worked in the international organisation for more than twenty years he had never worked in an organisation that appeared to have such a toxic culture as the Sydney affiliate. Some of the very visible symbols that met him included the 4 p.m. drinks cart that was wheeled around every afternoon (and at 3 p.m. on Fridays). His predecessor was charismatic and gregarious, and created an almost party-like atmosphere that also, unfortunately, bred toxicity to the extent that no one trusted anyone else in the organisation and many people actively sought to be disruptive.

One of the first things Leonard did was to banish the drinks cart and forbid all alcohol on the premises. As he expected, this was met with huge resistance but he was determined he needed to create a new set of symbols if he had any chance of influencing the organisational culture. Three years later when he left Australia for a different role, Leonard handed over a more disciplined and structured organisation than the one he had inherited.

Organisational mandate and financials

Irrespective of title or level of responsibility, as the most senior leader of an international affiliate you will be judged on the financial results and reporting of the affiliate. It is common for expatriate leaders to be promoted to GM/MD for the first time from 'non-finance' functional roles such as sales and marketing. As a result, it is not uncommon for those with such a background to be unfamiliar with the management and reporting of this data.

Outputs
- Clarity on financials, trading history, contribution to overall organisation and global reputation of the affiliate.

Questions
- What is the overall company situation — history, trading, reputation, financial history?

Where the business creates profitability and leverage points:
- Where does the money come from? Where does it go?
- Are there reserves being allocated for pet projects?
- What are the profit engines? How can they be accelerated?
- What are the expectations of stakeholders within the international organisation?
- Do you have agreement on the organisation's broad goals in the immediate and short term?

Actions
- Summarise all relevant information into a format that is easily accessible.
- Ensure an understanding of the local financial reporting requirements within two months of your arrival.

Working with your boss and peers

Part of an expat leader's success lies in how they communicate with their boss, who is invariably in a different geographical zone. In most cases you will also have a boss with whom you have not worked before. Therefore, developing a reporting rhythm where you have regular conversations is important.

When the overseas leader visits Australia they will usually conduct second- and third-level down interviews to meet employees. They will do this primarily to check the alignments with the reports they have been receiving and how those actions have been received. A common failure of expat leaders is not keeping their overseas leader up to date with insights and proposed actions.

Outputs

- Understand how to manage-up appropriately and how to get the best support and input from your leader.
- Clarify their expectations.
- Clarify their reporting requirements (.e. how often they will want to have a teleconference and site visits?)

Questions
Understanding the boss:

- How do they describe their style, needs, dislikes, etc.?
- How do others explain the boss' style, needs, dislikes, etc.?
- What does the boss expect of you — explicitly and implicitly?
- What balance between formality and informality is best in communication?
- What regular reports are expected and in what form — formal, informal, verbal or written?
- What are the boss' priorities and pressures?

Understanding your role:

- The extent of your role — where are the informal boundaries?
- Where does it fit in the overall strategy for their business?
- What are the elements for which you are responsible?
- Is there a business/departmental strategy? What are your first impressions of its clarity?
- Does it need reviewing?
- What are the annual targets and goals? How clear are the measurements?
- Is there any mismatch between budgets, targets and strategies?
- What are your delivery deadlines?

- How do expectations compare with current performance levels?
- Is a major leap in performance expected and, if so, what are the underlying reasons?
- What are the risk and compliance issues facing the organisation?

Understanding your peer group:
- What is the recent history of the group?
- What are their individual strengths and weaknesses?
- Where will you fit into this group (what is to be your role and stance)?
- What amount of socialising goes on in this group?

Actions
- Agree on reporting requirements, frequency and style.
- Suggest one-, two- and three-month objectives.
- Understand that the boss may want to have a closer managerial relationship with you initially to ensure you settle in. If this feels like micro-management, renegotiate after the first three months.
- Develop a list of learnings, insights, decisions and actions to communicate to the overseas leader.
- Prepare for updates around the broad areas of:
  - Here is the context I have found.
  - Here is what I have noticed about the organisation/culture/practices.
  - Here is what customers are telling me.
  - Here is how I would describe the leadership team and its members.
  - Here is what I plan on doing.

Understand your markets and customers

'Communication is the real work of leadership,' according to Nitin Nohria, Dean of Harvard Business School. A key transition hurdle expatriate leaders face is spending sufficient time in investing in relationships. Taking a week before officially starting to meet stakeholders not only displays a strong desire to invest in the relationship but shows you are proactive. Gaining the loyalty of customers is hard won and easily lost.

Having a clear stakeholder map including both internal (direct reports and key people) and external (key customers, customer groups, industry associations, key opinion leaders, government sectors and external vendors) allows the new leader to plan and schedule meetings ideally in the first week but certainly within the first month.

One of the great challenges when moving into a new market is how to quickly understand how the organisation, its products, services and people are perceived by the customers and key stakeholders. This information will be helpful in forming decisions and correlating reports from other sources. There is also a wonderful opportunity in the beginning of tenure for new leaders to establish good relationships with key and influential individuals and groups.

Outputs
- Clarify the external perceptions and your sales and service function's capability compared to expectations.

Questions
Customers:
- Who are strategically vital customers?
- Understand the recent history of KOLs (key opinion leaders).
- What is the company's external reputation as described by customers?
- Identify the most influential internal customers.
- What is the experience your customers have of the organisation?
- How do they assess your products and services and the overall customer service?
- How do they rate your organisation compared to your competitors?
- What would they have you do differently for them to remain loyal customers?
- What would they have you do so they would become advocates of your organisation?
- Does the company do any systematic external benchmarking?
- What is your view around the overall industry and where it is headed?
- What are the issues and implications facing the industry in the next couple of years?
- What would they like from the organisational leader over the next couple of years?
- Is there anything I can do to help them?

Partners:
- What is their perspective on the relationship they have in working with your organisation? How do they see the overall relationship progressing into the future?
- Where are the mutual successes between you and their organisation?
- What do they see as being the flaws of the organisation?

Suppliers:
- How difficult do your suppliers find it working with the organisation?
- Where are the barriers to a win–win relationship?
- How can you optimise the overall relationship so it becomes a fully conscious business relationship?

Key services such as accountants and legal services:
- What do your main service partners think of the state of the business?
- What concerns do they hold for the organisation in its current state and market?
- How do they rate your organisation relative to the overall market?

Outside analysts:
- What is their overall view of the market and your organisation in the market?

Association and member groups:
- What is the state of the overall industry?
- How does your organisation fare compared to your competitors?
- What are some of the potential regulatory or government changes that may impact the industry over the next couple of years?
- What is the process for members to seek committee representation?
- How influential is the association on the overall environment?

Industry-related stakeholders:
- What are some of the main issues facing the industry in Australia?
- What are the implications of those issues over the next couple of years?
- What is the stakeholders' view of the organisation as it stands within the industry?
- How are your competitors viewed in the industry?
- What should you focus on as an organisational leader in this industry over the next couple of years?
- Is there anything specific industry-related stakeholders need or want from you in your role in Australia?
- Is there anything you can do to help industry-related stakeholders?

Frontline staff:
These are the people who understand your business at a day-to-day tactical level. While they may never fully understand the overall strategy, they see clearly the impact the strategy and execution has on the customer. Their point of view is critical if you are to fully understand where the organisation sits in the marketplace.

- Identify the key influencers in the organisation (see Table 2).
- What is the experience in delivering the products and services to the customers?

- What difficulties arise within the organisation which impact service delivery?
- What are some of the frustrations sitting within the organisation and how might they be relieved?

Actions
- Spend quality time with important customers and your key stakeholders to establish and build a personal relationship.

The table below lists the traits of key influencers in an organisation. Quite often the most influential people do not carry the most senior title. Therefore it is worth investing the time to learn who they are.

Table 2: Key influencers[8]

People with expertise	Usually heads of functions or subject matter experts. They are called upon because of their knowledge and expertise.
People with history in the organisation	These people have been in the organisation for ten or more years, and in the case of a start-up, from day one. Their historical and tacit knowledge is immense and they hold the keys to understanding 'how things get done'.
History	People with history are often related to major decisions, successful product launches, relationships to key influences internationally or who have achieved a degree of legacy for some reason in the organisation.
Status	People with status are often in the more senior leadership roles or have achieved great notoriety or outcomes for the organisation.
People with power	The Darth Vaders of the organisation are those who have immense power and who use it to build their own fiefdoms. They are often charismatic but ultimately serve themselves.
The bean counters	They may not be accountants but are people who control resources, such as budgets, rewards, head count, access to information, access to perks and access to car parks.

Susan had heeded the advice given to her and organised a pre-start date two weeks in advance of her official start date. Once her husband and kids were settled in she organised to have a series of meetings in and outside of the office in Sydney.

With the help of the local Human Resources Director she had one-on-one meetings with all of her future direct reports. Susan referred to this week as 'doing the missionary work' (i.e. sowing the seeds that will later flower). She was able to have a cordial, friendly meeting with them, got to understand their history and asked for the business plans for their various functions so she could read them before her official start date. She also took the opportunity to briefly talk about herself, her background and her preferred leadership style.

Through the help of her direct reports she organised to meet the key customer groups and KOLs (key opinion leaders) that influenced the sector in which they operated. Three CEOs of her major customers were very pleasantly surprised she had come to see them before officially starting. One of them commented to her that, given her predecessor appeared to actively ignore their customers, he was pleasantly surprised and optimistic that she was taking a very different path. She took the opportunity to understand his perception of their service, product delivery and where they stood in the overall market. Susan was pleased when she received an email two days later from the same customer saying he valued her visit and looked forward to working closely with her while she was in Australia.

Understanding the current leadership team

Your performance as a leader will be judged upon the performance you inspire in your team. Often a mandate for new leaders is to make an assessment of the performance and potential of the existing team and then support that assessment through action. It is critical in the first few months that you establish an unbiased and well-informed perspective about the team.

One of the most interesting aspects of observing a new leader and their new team is watching how long it takes for each party to understand how best to work together. Given how important the impact and influence of this is across the organisation, it makes sense to accelerate the process of understanding how best to work with each other.

Dave Ulrich is well known for designing a new leader's assimilation process that overcomes some of these queries and has the team learn this information in the first week of the new leader commencing. Organisations such as Honeywell, Amgen and GE have embraced this process to be used with new incoming leaders. An adapted version is available on the website at www.foreignerincharge.com.

Engaging with your direct reports and exploring the following points can deliver a range of benefits.

Outputs

- Understand the overall history of key personnel, the preceding leader and any relevant highs and lows relating to leadership in the affiliate.
- Gain insight into the overall organisation and to start sowing the seeds for where you want to take the organisation and how you want to operate as their leader.
- Have a clear understanding of the external reputation of the leadership capability within the local organisation (regardless of whether this represents reality).
- Have a perspective on individual and team capability to deliver as required.
- Understand the actions required and in what timeframe.

Questions

Role/background:

- How was your predecessor perceived — why and where has s/he gone?
- Who else applied for your role? Are they still within the organisation? Was the team expecting someone else to get the position?
- Are there other newly appointed senior staff?

Your team:

- What does the team's last performance review show?
- What are their individual strengths and weaknesses?
- What do they do as a team? Do you understand their individual roles and interactions?
- How well do they operate as a team?
- How do they collaborate together?
- How robust are the conversations?
- Can they deliver the strategy?
- How good at execution are they?
- How are they perceived by people within the company?
- How are the team perceived by people outside the company (e.g. customers, suppliers)?
- What, in the team's view, are the key problems and opportunities?
- Are they happy? How's morale (and what are the reasons for this)?

Questions to ask direct reports:

- Tell me about your history in this organisation.
- Tell me about your function.
- Tell me about the business for your function over the next two years.
- Tell me about the issues your function faces.
- What is your view of the organisational strategy as it currently stands?

- Where are the potential issues facing the organisation locally?
- If you were in charge what would you be doing over the next six to twelve months?
- Who do you think are important stakeholders that I need to meet over the next couple of weeks?
- Ideally what would you like from me over the next couple of years?

Questions they will want answered:
- How do you make decisions?
- How inclusive or not are you in consulting your team?
- How do you like to receive information?
- How will they know when you are happy/unhappy with their performance?
- What are your prior successes?
- What is your family situation?

Actions
- Conduct one-on-one interviews to gain insight into the roles, functions, business plans, processes and experience of the history of the organisation.
- Write up a summary of the leadership capability that is said to be true and aim to validate this within two to three months of your arrival.
- Aim to fill in a capability map of the overall leadership team and each individual within three months of your arrival.
- Deliberate what kind of leadership is required from you to effectively lead the current team.
- Conduct a new leader assimilation exercise with your team.

Understanding the organisational culture

If the definition of culture is 'the way we do things around here' (whether consciously or not), then a leader needs to actively look and learn how things are done to understand an organisation's culture. Of course, for experienced leaders this definition of culture is far too simple. The way things are done around here is influenced by a broad range of variables such as organisational history, key personalities, systemic structures, hidden barriers, said and unsaid rules of behaviour, performance management or lack of, remuneration plans or lack of, previous leaders and their legacies and a whole range of other variables in the external environment.

Edgar Schein is regarded as one of the early experts in organisational culture. He talks about three important levels the leader needs to understand: symbols, norms and assumptions. [9]

Symbols are the signs people see in organisations such as logos, pictures, style of dress, hierarchy, time of starting and finishing work, celebrations of success, rewarding behaviours, promotions into key positions, speed of decisions and execution on key promises. Symbols distinguish one organisation from another as well as one country from another.

Norms are the social rules that encourage the preferred behaviour and the behaviour that is frowned upon. These norms are can be both said and unsaid. In sophisticated and mature organisations employees have clear performance agreements and appraisal reviews on a six-monthly basis. This is very overt — that is, said. However, there are also many unsaid, less overt norms in an organisation such as who gets what car space or which business function unit gets what perks. Leaders need to understand what norms elicit loyalty, scorn, approval or even promotion.

Assumptions are the unsaid but very strong beliefs underpinning an organisation. Because they are so strong they're often taken for granted and resisted when challenged. Some people call these the truths; however, they are only made truths when they are given oxygen to live on. A typical assumption in underperforming organisations is that 'leaders talk but don't take action' so there is no point in offering up ideas that might enable change. Like all assumptions there is a hint of truth in these or a historical reason why at some stage that assumption may have been true. This does not mean the assumption holds strong over time.

Our experience suggests there is a fourth aspect to organisational culture: **language**. Every organisation has a narrative. Key words or phrases are used to describe particular patterns, behaviours, norms or even symbols. Stories live in the organisation and underpin assumptions and often explain past behaviours. Tapping into the organisational language or narrative can really help you understand what lies behind the culture. One successful expat from the United Kingdom tapped into a regular phrase he heard in the organisation that went along the lines of 'If you want to trust something will get done, do it yourself'. He turned that phrase into 'I trust you enough that you will do your job and that everyone here will do what they say they will do'. This had a catalytic effect of accelerating collaboration and allowing everyone to minimise the micro-controlling of each other.

After two months in the organisation Susan sat down to reflect on everything she had learnt. She poured through all her notes and felt she had a strong grasp of the organisation history, business plans, where the organisation stood in the market, reasons for decisions being made in the past and the potential aspiration for where the organisation could be in the future. At a superficial level this all felt quite familiar to her. Having spent twelve years in Chicago in head office she understood the business and its operations. The local affiliate in Australia operated along very similar lines.

However, at a deeper level she now understood that it was quite different. The way Australians worked, the mindset they brought to their job, the way they dealt with each other, the deference or lack of deference they held for their leaders, all felt palpably different to her experience in Chicago. Susan realised what she was thinking about could be summed up by the word 'culture'. Essentially, the culture in the Australian organisation was quite different to the US head office organisation. With that she also understood she needed to do more work with the leadership team to make sure they, as a collective entity, were influencing the broader culture.

Outputs
- An initial understanding of the culture and values of the organisation.
- An understanding of the current state of the organisation and what this requires of you in resetting the culture.
- Assuming the survey instrumentation is of high quality or is externally benchmarked, these give a good insight into where the organisation is relative to its competitors.

Questions
- How are things done?
- How are the decisions made — through formal or informal processes?
- What kind of behaviour is really valued?
- How bureaucratic/collaborative/achievement orientated is it?
- What is the pace of acceptance of change?
- What are the espoused values? (Is the espousal merely lip service, or a genuine and integral part of the corporate or local culture?)
- What gets priority?
- What/who gets rewarded?
- What are the 'hero' stories?
- What do you see around the organisation — furnishings, signs, posters etc.?
- What are the symbols you notice?

Actions
- Be able to articulate how people behave and with what consequences.

- Be in a position to assess the organisation's culture by month four either anecdotally or through a formal process by using a culture tool such as The Leadership Circle's Culture Survey™.
- Read organisation documentation such as climate surveys, engagement scores and other HR metrics and discuss these documents in detail with the document owner.
- Plan to formally assess the organisational culture using a diagnostic tool such as The Leadership Circle's Culture Survey™.[10]

When Matt took over from his predecessor, Peter, there was a month's handover. Peter had been in the role for over ten years and his ongoing presence on the fifth floor of the building perpetuated the impression of him continuing to be the CEO. As with most leaders, Peter's office was a reflection of him through various photographs and memorabilia decorating the walls.

Matt was asked by his coach to think about where he was going to sit for the month Peter was still onsite. Matt understood the importance of symbolism. He also understood that, during the first couple of weeks, everybody watches the new leader to see what they do so as to gain insight into their habits and personality. As a result, Matt realised that having a conversation with Peter about where he would sit was important.

Together they decided that although it would cause a bit of hassle, removing Peter's large desk from the office and replacing it with two desks where they would work together would create a very strong symbol that Peter was handing over the office to Matt. Once Peter left, Matt took out both desks and put in a new desk and changed the photographs on the wall to ones reflecting his personality and interests, thus creating a symbol that there was a new leader.

How to get started

Every leader understands the need to secure early wins in their first two months. This allows you to prove you have listened to issues raised, to show you are a person of action and influence and to justify your appointment by proving your competence. One of our clients, Becki from the United States, called this process 'painting the lobby'. The term comes from the US health care industry where the private hospital systems compete for every dollar and have to set up their hospitals to look like five-star hotels. Therefore, when a new CEO takes over a private hospital they paint the hospital lobby to upgrade it to the next level of five-stardom!

Whether you actively take on a project in your first couple of weeks to illustrate where you want to lead or you do nothing at all, you have 'painted the lobby'. Your actions are visible and the shadow you cast, by the mere fact you are the leader, is equally visible. During the 'look, listen and learn' phase of meeting with each key insight group you need to be attuned to what kind of 'paint the lobby' project you would like to undertake that is visible and worthwhile to the organisation. Even though it may take six to twelve weeks for you to convene the leadership team and to co-create and articulate the new strategy, you cannot afford to wait for that outcome before you start securing early wins.

In an earlier case study I mentioned Leonard, who arrived to a toxic culture. His 'paint the lobby' project was banning alcohol in the organisation. Everything else he did in the first two months was aligned with showing he wanted to bring more discipline into the organisation, so when it came to announcing the strategy no one was in any doubt that things were about to change. Another leader who arrived at GE Australia from an overseas position also felt that a stronger degree of discipline was needed. In his first town hall meeting he announced 'there is a new sheriff in town'. He then asked for all employment contracts and sales compensation agreements to be reviewed to be more aligned with the upcoming strategy.

Outputs
- Impact, creation of energy and results focus.

Questions
- What are all the threats to the business and its ability to thrive? These are often the key to the discovery of opportunities for 'quick wins.'
- What are the things you notice as a person with fresh eyes that strike you as curious as to process or practice?

Actions
- Hone your ability to detect hidden opportunities.
- Generate a multitude of opportunities for 'quick wins'. Quick wins might include negotiating an expanded agreement with a key customer, curtailing new-product development in weak categories, and launching a comprehensive productivity initiative to match a competitor's lower costs.
- Avoid the trap of trying to fix every problem in an attempt to show you are in charge. Pick and choose your quick hits, and be selective. You can become so bogged down in operational detail you lose sight of the big picture.

Shannon took over as leader of the organisation from a position in the United Kingdom. His reputation in the sporting industry was strong. The local organisation he took over had a proud history but recently had been less successful. He immediately noticed that the organisation had promoted individual 'stars' rather than the overall team. In one of his opening addresses to the organisation, Shannon retold the famous story of Alex Ferguson of Manchester United, arguably the most successful football coach in history, who fired David Beckham, arguably the most famous player in history, from the team. Alex said at the time and many times since that no player is bigger than the team. In retelling the story to his audience Shannon said, 'I don't want to have my David Beckham moment but I have no hesitation in doing that as no one is bigger than this organisation'.

Over the next two weeks Shannon very actively examined the teams and levels of teamwork in the organisation. One 'star' resigned of their own accord within a month. Two years later the organisation was starting to enjoy levels of success it had never previously encountered.

Not all 'paint the lobby' projects are successful. Leaders who do not take time to fully understand the organisational culture inadvertently create symbols the organisation will ultimately reject.

George arrived in Sydney from South Korea. An Indian by birth, and educated in America, he was a self-declared 'action man'. Within one month of arrival he had every piece of artwork removed across the whole building and replaced with commissioned artworks which were highly evocative and competitive style photographs. Each photo image had a tag line blazing across it, stating 'The hunt for 300'. Without taking time to understand the organisational history or strategy, George had decided the new business target was to achieve $300 million in revenue within twelve months. This was almost double where they were currently sitting.

Inadvertently, George's 'paint the lobby' project meant that overnight his reputation became that 'this man is completely mad and devoid of all reality'. In his removal of all the existing artwork he also displayed what was interpreted as disrespect to the organisational history and the people that had gone before him. George left the business within nine months.

How to keep building the family foundations

Having a solid foundation at home is critical if you are to be effective in the workplace. It is important that you and your partner recognise and talk about the fact that the crucial first period in the new role will demand unusual amounts of your time and attention. Because of that, you must make a real effort to talk over and share your impressions, concerns and reactions with your partner.

Outputs
- Shared understanding and goals with your partner/family.
- Satisfying and happy relationships.

Questions
- What are your personal goals?
- What support do you need from those closest to you to make them happen?
- What planning do you need to undertake to ensure achievement?
- How are these aligned with the goals and priorities of your partner/family?

Actions
- Take time to explain to your partner what is going on — share your feelings.
- Encourage your partner to reciprocate and make time to listen constructively.
- Share people problems and issues as they arise — don't bottle them up, and remember that first impressions matter.
- Try to make sure your partner meets some of the new people as appropriate — at least ensure s/he meets the key players!
- Practise positive and healthy lifestyle habits especially when under the additional pressures of 'settling in'.

Graham and Rachael were nervous about moving to Australia from Yorkshire via Taiwan. In reality Graham was nervous, albeit he never shared that with Rachael. She was of the view that they were sacrificing a lot to follow his career, and she often reminded him of that. He felt that she yearned for her former life in Yorkshire, close to her family and life as she knew it. At least in Taiwan, where he'd taken a role as a Sales Director, they were in a really 'foreign' country with everything appearing new and interesting. Having home help in the form of a full-time live-in maid offered Rachael a true taste of expatriate life, which she enjoyed.

Three years later Graham was confident that coming to Australia would offer his career the step to a larger role in a larger market, a perfect step towards the Managing Director role he desired. He was nervous, though, that Rachael would not enjoy the experience. From month one in Australia, Graham got stuck into his new role and enjoyed the challenges it brought. But Rachael never settled. With that, the children never settled. As Graham got busier at work his family seemed to get unhappier at home. Eventually Rachael brought everything to a head: either Graham got a transfer back to the United Kingdom or she was leaving without him. Graham resigned his position very sorrowfully. Graham said later he wished he had taken more time to settle in his family in the early stages of their Australian assignment.

9

THE DECIDE PHASE

Skills needed

At an individual level, you need to be clear on what is needed, why and when.

At a leadership team level, the skill is to gain leadership team buy-in and collaboration when arriving at the major decisions.

At the organisational level, the skill is to be seen to lead.

Key question

What decisions have to be made to lead this organisation?

Key outcome

Purpose.

After eight weeks in her new role in Sydney, Susan was ready to bring her leadership team together to deliberate and decide the collective future for the business. She understood this would not be a one-off event but rather a series of meetings over the next couple of weeks to build up the collective vision and strategy for the organisation.

Her manager José had left her alone in the first six weeks to get her feet under the table and to understand the business in its broadest context. She knew he would be looking for her insights into how she was going to lead the business forward. Again the voice of her old mentor rang in her ears: 'Susan, the role of a leader is to lead. Always make sure you're providing clarity and direction for the people you lead, even if they are also leaders.' She went about organising a series of leadership team meetings over the next month starting with a 'purpose' workshop.

Every leader needs to lead an organisation to somewhere. Whether there is a burning platform for change, the company is in a transition from start-up to sustainability or myriad other potential changes, the leader is responsible for leading their organisation *somewhere.* Creating clarity and a sense of direction is one of the key roles and skills required of a new leader.

When an expat leader arrives in a new country they need to simultaneously co-create the direction for the organisation and the leadership team. This added complexity often feels like it is slowing them down. However, taking the time and effort to focus the leadership team on its collective role as well as the direction for the organisation is essential. The narrative following many failed expat leaders is that they never took the time to either understand the organisation's context or to set one for the future.

There are hundreds of books on the role of a leadership team, the role of strategy, and the importance of direction. This book does not seek to cover that territory in detail, however our experience shows attending to and reiterating the fundamentals is an important learning point for every expat leader. Let's start with the leadership team.

The leadership team

The importance of understanding each member of the leadership team and their performance together has also been highlighted as an integral part of the new expatriate leader's first-quarter plan in Chapter 8. This section will look at the immediate pattern and content of meetings you should undertake with the leadership team.

In their book *The Wisdom of Teams*, Katzenbach and Smith skilfully point out that most teams are in fact working groups.[1] A working group regularly comes together to report on the output of their function. They report to one single leader but rarely have any communal output in common. A classic example of a working group is the shared service function which may include services, human resources, auditors and legal.

A cross-functional leadership team sitting in a country affiliate, however, can and should be an effective leadership team. Katzenbach and Smith also observe that a leadership team needs to take the time to consider what they actually have in common, what outputs they are collectively responsible for and how they are going to measure the collective responsibility. Peter Hawkins, who wrote *Leadership Team Coaching: Developing collective transformational leadership*, says 'A leadership team needs to ask itself what it is collectively responsible for other than delivering only numbers. Once it finds a unique collective responsibility it can then start focusing on becoming a team.'[2]

Many leadership teams fail to ask these questions and later a sense of ambiguity or, worse still, dysfunctionality creeps in. The root cause is often traced back to a lack of core purpose and clarity on the roles and responsibilities needed to deliver that core purpose. Taking time to make the obvious overt pays dividends so that nothing is covert.

Every team starts again when a new member joins. When the newest member of the team happens to be the new leader, the team slows down, if not stalls, until the leader fully takes the helm. Therefore, having the conversation of 'What are we doing together as a leadership team?' or 'What is our purpose in leading this organisation?' is very useful and fruitful.

Purpose meeting

Between weeks four and eight you need to hold a meeting with your leadership team. We refer to this as the 'purpose meeting' — other sources may refer to this as creating a burning ambition or a burning platform. This meeting is a significant symbol of leadership for you. It is an active demonstration of the expectation of leadership. How you position the meeting, its purpose and your expectations will set the tone. (See 'Opening the off-site' handout on the website.)

A purpose meeting is typically a one- or two-day offsite event, depending on how much time the team wants to spend together socially. Teams who are new to each other or who have not previously worked together closely find it valuable to use two days, with an overnight stay offsite, as it allows them to spend extended time together. It allows for connections and relationship building as there is space for simple conversations to take place that uncover personal insights that may not have been previously shared.

A typical agenda includes the following:

Are we a team?
There is a choice to make about being a team or being a working group. The benefits of each are loud and clear but starkly different. For more information see www.foreignerincharge.com.

If we decide to be a team, what is our purpose?
A true team delivers more than just the numbers. While a leadership team will always be judged upon its financial results, getting to those results can involve many different strategies and execution modes. Having a purpose other than just numbers allows for creativity, leadership, personal growth and potential transformation.

This highlights the importance of the leadership team tapping into something more powerful and purposeful than the traditional business transactions as a starting point to defining organisational values and behaviours. Given the recent phenomena of the Simon Sinek 'why, what, how' talk at Ted.com it would appear that many others all over the globe would agree.[3]

Mission and vision

Most affiliates of international businesses adopt the head office mission and vision statements. Multinationals have usually decided what markets or industries they wish to operate in. The role for the local leadership team, then, is identifying the local nuances relating to mission and vision (e.g. a discussion about where the organisation needs to get to over the next three to five years and making the vision part of that conversation).

Broad commercial objectives

You will have received a mandate from your boss and therefore the objectives will flow as a result. The leadership team need to understand the collective objectives upon which they will be measured and towards which the organisation needs to be led.

Strategy development

The phase of growth the organisation finds itself in will determine to what level strategic development conversations are required. The baseline discussion is examining the current strategy and checking for how well it has been executed. For most purpose meetings this conversation results in mapping out the work needing to be done.

Rules of engagement

For any team starting out working together or restarting with a new team member, clarifying the ideal ways of working together, or the 'rules of engagement', is very useful. This is not a fluffy conversation. It is a clear and practical discussion about how the team wants and needs to work together. Items covered should include the current types of meetings versus what is required; the way meetings are conducted; frequency and length; agenda preparation and management; and the behaviours expected from each other in and outside those meetings.

Strategy development meetings

After the purpose meeting a series of strategy review meetings are held to deliberate, debate and co-create the strategic direction. The level of analysis, investigation and sharing of information is decided upon and responsibilities allocated.

Given the normal difficulty with finding a date on which every member of the leadership team can attend, it is important the next series of meetings is set in everyone's diaries and agreed to before departing from the purpose meeting. It is a sign of your leadership intent to commit to this process, an indication of the team's commitment to each other and to the role of leadership in the organisation. There will always be competing agendas and 'biting alligators' that will compete with time in everyone's diary. However, the role of leaders is to lead. Setting clarity and direction is the output of strong leadership.

George arrived in Sydney from New Zealand. Even though New Zealand and Australia are geographically very close, many Kiwis find the transition to Australia surprisingly difficult. George was a very charismatic and strong people leader. He heeded the advice and did not jump to conclusions regarding what the organisation would need. He spent a lot of time talking to people, visiting customers in their offices, spending time in the field with sales representatives and holding focus groups to understand where the organisation was at and where it needed to be.

George was applauded for making this effort and within a short period of time had developed a reputation for being interested in people and for listening to their concerns. He had also spent time with his leadership team to co-create the team's operating rhythm to allow them to meet regularly and appropriately to discuss the most important issues.

After three months his review was very positive. However, two months later, George's boss in Chicago started getting feedback through the back channels that things were not quite as rosy in Sydney as originally thought. While George had taken a long time to listen, he had not actually given any sense of direction or intended direction. Various strategic initiatives were slowing down as people were waiting for new direction from the leadership team and had put projects related to the existing strategy on hold until they heard otherwise.

Although George exhibited great skills in listening and understanding the context, he was failing to deliver on the most important leadership skills of giving clarity and direction.

This book is not designed to be a strategy book — there are many great ones already available. However, the role of leaders is to lead and the key skill involved is giving clarity and setting direction, so the following gives some guidance in this regard.

After the purpose meeting, the next series of important meetings involve debating the strategy. Your mandate will determine the kind of strategy needed. As we saw in Chapter 6 there are different stages of organisational development and phases the business will go through, from start-up to wind down.

For most multinational organisations with an Australian affiliate, the broad strategy is decided at a regional, if not global, level. A pharmaceutical organisation, for example, will decide to launch particular products in each country once they have been tested in one location such as North America or the United Kingdom. The launch in Australia will be dependent on the Therapeutic Goods Administration (TGA) and the level of reimbursement received. There are specific strategies that need to be deployed relating to reimbursement issues only. For other industries, strategy deployment and product launches will be dependent upon market conditions, market penetration, partnership agreements, competitive advantages or lack of, key organisational skill sets or lack of, and the level of financial investments required and available to launch new initiatives.

For some organisations, getting external help from a strategy consulting house is an essential part of strategy development. For other organisations, the strategy intelligence lies in-house and third-party intelligence support may come in the form of accounting or banking support, marketing or niche marketing intelligence or creative agency design support.

One-page visual plan

One of the most useful outputs from these meetings is a one-page visual plan that captures the main strategic outputs and actions. This will be useful to hold everyone accountable but more importantly to share with the broader organisation. Australians are genuinely interested in the contextual reasons behind decisions and want to understand why strategic decisions are made.

While there is no right or wrong way to create such a visual plan, there are sections that are regularly included. A printout is available at the website (see www.foreignerincharge.com).

Scenario planning

One very useful activity for a leadership team to undergo when creating or reviewing a strategic direction is to identify a range of scenarios which may be encountered and agree on the decision-making process they would undertake if the scenarios became reality.

Christopher led his team through a series of conversations regarding potential operation expenditure cuts the organisation could undergo in the upcoming twelve months. Starting at 10 per cent OPEX cuts, they worked through four different scenarios if cuts were at 10, 20, 30 or even 40 per cent. What he found was the team had no problem deciding strategies or tactics if faced with a 10 per cent cut. However, as the scenarios progressed from 10 per cent up to 40 per cent the team realised the decisions made at a 10 per cent cut could not be the same as those needed for a 30 or 40 per cent cut. The team were forced to step back from their functional roles and take a view across the business. They were forced to become both very creative and yet pragmatic in how they would deal with scenarios for a 30 or 40 per cent cut.

In the debrief following their session, the leadership team admitted this was the first meeting in their careers that had forced them to actively detach from their functional leadership responsibilities and take a very strong, business-wide leadership role in making strategic decisions. When the leadership team was able to operate at a company-wide level, decisions were made to best serve the entire organisation which may have actively impacted their own function.

Christopher commented on the insights he gained about each member of the team, how they naturally operated and how he could potentially help develop them as leaders. Everyone agreed this was a very different but constructive way of creating a strategic direction for the organisation. Ironically, a year later, when cuts were announced at 28 per cent, the leadership team were prepared and acted swiftly.

Communication cascading meetings

Once the strategy has been deliberated the last meeting or series of meetings focuses on how to communicate the information through the organisation. Organisations often have natural communication platforms built into their rhythm, such as end-of-month or end-of-quarter town hall meetings, regular weekly whole-of-company meetings, functional offsites or the use of a range of technologies to communicate with everybody simultaneously.

Whatever platforms are available, the leadership team needs to utilise them for best impact. The type of strategy developed and the current state of the business will determine the degree of urgency when communicating the strategy. From an Australian leadership perspective, expat leaders have commented Australians tend to be very pragmatic and desire substance over style and truth over illusion. This means that if there is bad news to announce then ... announce it.

There is also an increasing desire to have information provided through conversations rather than formal written announcements. The rise of video and social media to keep people informed also provides excellent platforms for real-time feedback. The trick is to identify and effectively utilise the communication platforms that best suit the needs of the audience rather than the leader's preference.

Scott was preparing for his first whole-of-company meeting three months after his arrival to the organisation. The event was the annual national sales conference, an event traditionally attended by all members of the organisation.

Scott had taken the leadership team through a strategic review process and while they had not arrived at final conclusions, the indicators were relatively obvious as to what direction lay ahead. For the first time, their previous cash cow products would be the target of active competition. The analysis projected a decline in profits over the next three years. The pipeline of products was at least eighteen months away and therefore there was going to be a cash flow issue within the coming eighteen months. This naturally would have an impact on the organisation, its strategy, full employment capability and other planned market initiatives. However, the leadership team had not finalised its strategic position and had not gained approval from the regional head office.

Scott, an experienced expat leader who'd had executive roles in three other countries before arriving to Australia, understood the importance of clear communication and sowing the seeds before announcing major news. Rather than avoiding the issue, he decided to flag what was going to come over the next three months. In his presentation he talked about the great success the affiliate had experienced in the preceding five years. He discussed that in the handover meetings with his predecessor, he understood loud and clear nothing was broken. In fact, the organisation was currently in a good state. He cleverly used the metaphor of a captain sailing a yacht in the ocean — it was currently in calm waters but the captain knew the storms were coming. He talked to the organisation about preparing and the importance of adaptability.

When it came to announcing budget cuts and constraints the organisation was ready and accepted the strategy as this was not an unfamiliar notion.

Practices with the leadership team

Recently I observed a three-day annual planning session, held in Hong Kong, for a multinational business. Fifteen people had flown in for the event including the top nine leaders for Asia. At the end of the meeting I asked the nine leaders, 'What are your top three focus points for this year?' I got 27 different answers to the question. Such lack of clarity of the message and the resulting disparate focus leads to a questioning of the exercise's value. Our experience suggests this is not unusual.

One of the more important areas for leaders to get right in the decide phase is what we collectively call 'practices with the leadership team'. This is a collection of relatively obvious but not well done practices that, when implemented, ensure the team is collectively aligned. Following is a discussion of these practices, beginning with clarity around the team's priorities.

Ensure the leadership team is clear on priorities

This sounds obvious but due to the nature of multinational organisational matrix structures, leadership team members often have a collection of priorities at functional, national and global levels. This can be very confusing and in some cases puts them into competition with local priorities.

It is important that you take time to ensure every leader in the local leadership team is clear on the priorities at a local level, on what this means for their functional priorities, and about what is expected from them as a leader in terms of execution. If every country leader just did that much, most organisations would be far more successful!

Cement the operating rhythm

Why do teams meet at all? Meetings consume a lot of time, especially if you consider that most team members, when surveyed, suggest meetings are a waste of time. Despite this limitation, meetings can be valuable. They contribute to generating collective thinking on issues, possible solutions, addressing performance-based issues, providing updates on progress and giving insights for reasons of recent success. When used properly they also provide safe forums for members to seek help or for peers to address underperformance in a trusting environment. Therefore, it makes sense to use meetings as a mechanistic way to accelerate team performance. Yet, many team leaders either do not or are unsure as to how.

Here are some of the comments made by team members when the challenge to attend meetings arises:

- 'We are all so busy here we couldn't possibly meet more than monthly or every quarter.'
- 'I can't possibly take my people off the road for a meeting.'
- 'These people are senior leaders or directors, they should know what to do without spending time in meetings.'

Yet, whenever we read about successful organisations or high-performing teams the key underlying accelerator to success is regular and constructive dialogue. Avoidance of unproductive meetings is understandable; the challenge is to ensure they are valuable. Having an efficient and effective operating rhythm facilitates this.

In working with expat leaders, one of the first assessments we encourage them to do is to understand the team's 'operating rhythm'. This is the overall rhythm of meetings the leadership team will attend in the course of a business cycle. An effective meeting schedule or operating rhythm is made up of a series of different meetings with different agendas and timeslots:

- annual planning meeting of two to three days
- quarterly meeting to review key milestones and goals of one or more days
- monthly business review session (including core projects) of half a day
- weekly/bi-weekly business updates of one to three hours
- a 'huddle' meeting (midweek or even daily) of five to twenty minutes.

Organisational leadership teams (as opposed to functional teams) will also have meeting points that cover:

- annual budgets
- marketing/brand reviews
- talent management reviews
- international visits
- potential acquisition activities
- reviewing the way the leadership team operates as a team.

Create and instil a decision-making protocol

A recurring issue for leadership teams as they develop their performance is how decisions get made within the team. The leader's style and the capability of the leadership team can influence the range of decision-making processes at a group level from unilateral to unanimous.

It is important to take time to actively decide which decisions will be made by which method (i.e. which will be by consensus, which will be functionally led and which lie at the sole discretion of the leader). With that comes a concept that is often referred to as 'DAI'. This is a useful framework for leaders and leadership teams to use in accelerating the decision-making process.

D stands for who actually holds the rights for this decision and who will be making that decision. From many conversations at leadership team level it may be unclear who actually holds the decision. For cross-functional teams this is a regular frustration. Being able to say who holds the 'D' in this conversation clarifies who will ultimately make the decision.

A is for those who provide advice in the conversation. There may be people in the room who have an opinion or expertise and provide advice — however, they don't hold the decision rights. Again, make it clear that their advice is welcome but ultimately somebody else makes the decision.

I stands for inform. When a decision is being made there are people who need to be informed about it. At a leadership team level, the role is to make sure the decision is executed or enacted upon. Everyone should have the opportunity to understand why the decision was made, however there is no excuse for someone not executing the decision because they did not actually make the decision. People need to understand that not questioning the decision infers alignment.

Peter came to Sydney from Europe, where he worked before moving to the United States, and was now on a three-year assignment in Australia. In his leadership review at the six-month mark, some of the feedback he received was around the need for decision making to be clearer at a leadership team level.

The organisation Peter was leading had a pre-existing core leadership model which meant many decisions had to be consensus-driven or at least pre-agreed before being brought to the leadership team meeting. The ambiguity this caused resulted in raised frustrations among team members. Adopting the DAI framework gave everyone a common language and way of working together. Peter commented later that the simple act of being able to say, 'You hold the D, I am simply giving you my advice,' allowed decisions to be made with clarity and speed. Likewise, being able to say, 'In this project decision I hold the D and here's what I want to do,' also enabled clarity and speed.

Later feedback from the organisation was that the leadership team appeared to be very aligned and decisive. Within a year of Peter's arrival the organisation had a number of successful new product launches with market-leading penetrations and, at the same time, was listed in the top 50 places to work in Australia. Peter commented that having a leadership team that was clear on its role and able to act decisively was a contributor to both these great outcomes.

Lead through stories, signs and symbols

Many articles suggest human beings are more visual and auditory than anything else. People listen to stories and then watch for symbols that reinforce those stories. In a series of experiments in his lab, psychologist Paul Zak showed that when watching a short, sad story about a father and son, two interesting neurochemicals were produced:

- cortisol, which is produced when people feel distress and encourages them to pay attention to the story
- oxytocin, which promotes connection and care and encourages people to feel empathy.[4]

After experiencing the story, people who produced the most oxytocin were the most likely to give money, even to others they could not see. Neuroscientists have been able to demonstrate using MRI scanning that stories with key emotive elements and a climax/high point engage the brain in a way that releases oxytocin. Stories without these fundamentals — that is, without a climax and conclusion — do not engage the brain in the same way. Indeed, people ignore such stories.

As you might expect this explains why babies and puppies are used in advertising. When we see those lovely cute images our brain is engaged and releases oxytocin, which helps us to build trust with that brand and, of course, ideally buy the product.

Leaders who are not great at storytelling need to be really clear with symbols and signs across the organisation to enforce the new direction.

Steve came to Australia from the United Kingdom later becoming Vice President, Asia-Pacific and the Middle East for a leading software company. He found the creative use of three symbols had a catalytic effect on momentum and energy among the sales leaders. The motto of 'Think big, act fast and make it count' was used to reinforce the strategic direction he and the leadership team had developed. Posters and other visual reminders were created and displayed at vantage points all over the organisation. At key meetings throughout the following year agendas were set aligned with these three key themes. Later he created a series of internal videos that highlighted successful client interactions and how the business answered their needs. This all went back to reinforcing, 'Think big, act fast and make it count'.

Regularly assess the leadership team

In *Good to Great*, Jim Collins talks about getting the right people on the bus before driving off. Most expat leaders will naturally inherit a team as opposed to picking their own members, and while the temptation can be to assess the team very quickly, it normally takes between six and 24 weeks for you to establish a clear point of view as to the capabilities of their colleagues on the leadership team. Even then, you may not be in a position to act or remove somebody for a couple more months. Using the three-stage meetings (the purpose, strategy development and the communication cascading meetings) you will gain insights into everyone's capability, motivations and fit.

Having the right people in the right role is fundamental to building a high-performing leadership team. With this in mind, you need to take time out to assess each of the individual leadership team members against a robust framework. The following leadership team assessment questions provide a helpful process to give a snapshot of the team and its capability.

1. What does the organisation need of the leadership team?

Given that by this stage you will have received a mandate, gained an understanding of the organisational context and history and will have co-developed a strategic direction, you will be able to answer the question 'What does the organisation need of the leadership team?' This can appear to be abstract but in reality it is fundamental. One of the issues organisational leaders often face is that the people who have served the organisation well and brought it to its current place are not always the right people to take it through its next phase of development. This is even more important in the leadership team as the organisation will only go as fast as their capability allows.

The future direction of the organisation can guide you in understanding what the leadership team needs to deliver and therefore, the capability the leadership team requires. The mantra 'change the people or change the people' becomes very important here. If the dynamics of the organisation need to be different then the leadership team members need to lead differently. They either need to change the way they lead (and their associated behaviours) or you need to have new people in the leadership team.

2. What are the strengths and motivations of each individual?

Positive psychology and organisational behaviour research over the last three decades have helped us understand the importance of strengths. All of us have natural strengths as well as behavioural 'derailers'. A leader needs to understand their direct reports' natural strengths so they can be best utilised. Likewise, personal motivations are very important when setting a strategic direction for the organisation. In an ideal world the motivations at an individual level are aligned with the organisational purpose and therefore leaders are working to fully serve the organisational needs. Of course, this is not always the case. Taking time to understand the motivations of each team member at a personal and functional level will help you understand the alignment of those motivations to the organisation.

3. Who best fits this team?

There is a natural chemistry within the best teams. It is often hard to predict in advance but easy to understand with the benefit of hindsight. Understanding where the organisation is heading and the capability needed to deliver the outcome will help you understand who has the best fit for the desired leadership team.

Team fit comes out of past experience, mindset, perspective, personal values and biases. No one set of perspectives, mindsets or biases is the right one. Indeed, at different stages of an organisational evolution different fits are necessary. In a turnaround situation, best fit often comes with the ability to work with energy and in ambiguity.

In a 2013 study the Boston Consulting Group notes that one of the mistakes new CEOs make is to focus only on top talent when building their leadership team. The report suggests the leader needs to give equal weight to both the *contextual* and *interpersonal suitability* of each individual. The overall combination of team members will contribute to a high-performing team, not necessarily a team of high-performing individuals.[5]

Individuals see the world in different ways and therefore create strategies and execute those strategies in different ways. If the role of a leader is to lead and therefore give clarity and direction, the next level of leaders needs to be able to co-lead and execute that direction.

4. What are the timelines needed for performance in each role?

It is not essential that every role is at full performance immediately. Likewise a high-performing team is not necessarily made up of high-performing individuals in every role at the same time. Great leaders look to build champion teams as opposed to teams of champions. Understanding where each team member sits in terms of their current performance and relative to what the role requires of them, in conjunction with the three questions above, allows for mapping.

Using a leadership team assessment matrix

As part of assessing the leadership team, developing a matrix that maps performance potential against best fit for the role is a useful process to see where each team member sits. There are many variations on this model and they are all useful.

Taking time to understand the leadership team members' motivations is important to make sure they are led accordingly. The inputs to this grid have been gathered in the look, listen and learn phase (i.e. through interviews, watching them in action in functional meetings, in leadership team meetings, in creating a strategy and how they communicate across the group). Prior appraisals or any available 360-degree results are also useful inputs.

Even though you may have just arrived in Australia it is useful to remember you will get your next promotion based upon how successful the leadership team is under your stewardship. Making sure you spend time developing the team is crucial to ensure your success in the role. Figure 8 maps out each individual with a best fit for the role and perfor-

Energise	**Engage**
The person is in the right role but not performing at the right level. They may be new to the role, their capability may not have been developed yet, they might be in circumstances not encountered before and unsure as to what to do or they might not have been developed to the right level. Regardless, the decision is to keep them and help develop them to get to the right level. This takes time but the investment is worthwhile as this person brings the right level of talent, motivation and fit.	This is when the right person is in the right role and is performing well. You need to do everything in your power to keep them in this role as they will be a major positive influence across the organisation.
Exit	**Evolve**
This is when the person is in the wrong role and are underperforming. The decision is relatively quick and it is easy to exit a person either to a different role or out of the organisation. The time to figure this out may be elongated depending on the choices available and the person's history in the organisation. Helping them understand that while they have served the leadership team well in the past, your decision is that they will be unable to do so in the future given the circumstances in which the organisation now finds itself.	Someone is in the wrong role but is a good performer. It could be the need for their function has changed and their skill set no longer matches the future need. It could also be their strengths and motivations are better suited for a different role and therefore finding their right role on the leadership team is, over time, the right decision. The temptation to keep them in a current role is often strong. However, if the guiding question is 'What does the organisation need of the leadership team?' then the decision to keep the person in this role is purely a time-bound one.

Team fit (vertical axis) · Performance (horizontal axis)

Figure 8: Leadership team assessment

mance in the role. Using the questions the leader gets to analyse their strengths, their motivation, their fit and the time needed to make a decision on each individual.

Warning: Make decisions early

In a qualitative study in Australia over 850 commercial leaders were asked to identify their biggest regret in their leadership career. Over 90 per cent of them reported it was not acting fast enough on poor performance when they instinctively knew much earlier that the particular individual was not the right person for the team. The reasons given for the delay were varied:

- The individual in question was a nice person and therefore this clouded the leader's judgement.
- The leader wanted to get more information to validate their intuition and perception.
- The organisational structure and history created barriers for a fast decision on performance management.
- The organisational culture as a whole was soft on performance management.
- The leader was new to the organisation and did not want to be seen to be making hasty judgements so early in their assignment.
- There was a web of relationships across the organisation and the leader wasn't sure as to the overall implications of taking action on underperformance with a particular individual.

Irrespective of the reasons, the regret remained the same and the respondents all said that, given their time again they would act differently.[6]

What is the ideal time to act upon the leadership team?

There is no ideal time to get the leadership team in place but it makes sense to do this as early as possible. It is advised that you be clear as to the right people for the team somewhere between ten and fourteen weeks after commencement. At this stage, the leadership team has collaborated in creating the strategy and you have had enough time to get insight into the level of exhibited performance needed into the future.

When Sean arrived in Australia to take over a telecommunications business, he'd had experience of running organisations in twelve different countries. Internationally he was recognised as a world-class leader, but for a range of reasons outside his control it still took him eleven months to get in place the leadership team he actually wanted. Because of this, a level of ambiguity and confusion set in at the leadership team level. This had to be actively managed and explained once Sean got his team in place.

Common communication platforms

There are continually evolving mechanisms for communications. Table 3 outlines some of the more common platforms that can be helpful in connecting with your people, both those within the leadership team and across the whole organisation.

Table 3: Communication platforms

Description	Pros	Cons
Town hall/group meetings Gathering of all company (or location-specific people) with the potential of electronically streaming to other locations where people are collectively gathered.	• Announcements/information sharing of organisational significance. Useful in ensuring everyone receives the same information at the same time from the same source. • Provides the opportunity to ask questions. • Might be the rare opportunity for employees to have direct access to senior leaders. • Can also be recorded for future use and reference.	Potential for people to be passive if there is not an active feedback mechanism in place (e.g. don't presume just because people have been 'told' that they have heard and understood what you intended).
Stand-up meeting • Usually conducted with an intact team located together. • Short 5–10 minute meeting held with everyone standing up (this ensures the meeting is short and keeps to time).	Catch up with hot topics, issues that need immediate attention, place for people to ask for help. Ensures everyone is informed and current.	Take care not to let this expand into a 'reporting of tasks' which can expand the time and limits value.
Group email Written communication electronically shared with all on the distribution list.	• Timely and immediate, which shares the same information with everyone at the same time. • Good as a follow-up or lead-in to support other communication platforms (e.g. can be a summary of other forums such as town hall meetings or as a lead-in to stand-up, business unit, team meetings).	• There is email overload. People may not read it. Those who do could misunderstand. • It can be seen as impersonal. Sensitive information is easy shared. • Doesn't easily allow for questions to be asked.

Description	Pros	Cons
Kick-off/launch meetings • Held at the beginning of a cycle (e.g. sales year or for an event, program). • Usually attended by all stakeholders from the local organisation and often regional and international representatives.	• Powerful symbol in setting culture and approach. • Set and share performance, strategy information. • Platform for showcasing and celebrating individual and group achievements and expectations.	• Potential for people to be passive if there is not an active feedback mechanism in place (e.g. don't presume just because people have been 'told' that they have heard and understood what you intended).
Retreats/away days Day/days spent offsite with colleagues (e.g. leadership, functional, project teams).	• Allows for concentration on agenda without office distractions. • Staying offsite allows for social and incidental conversation and connection that facilitates relationship building.	• Agenda can be sidelined if facilitation is not managed tightly. • Dysfunctional tendencies (team and individual) can limit effectiveness if not addressed and managed well. This can be in the meeting room (e.g. ineffective team dynamics) or lack of self-regulation in individual behaviour.
Team/business unit meetings • Scheduled regularly (e.g. quarterly, monthly, fortnightly) with intact, cross-functional teams. • People attend physically or may conference if appropriate.	Provides time-efficient mechanism for sharing information and addressing relevant issues shared by the attending group.	• Agenda can be sidelined if facilitation is not managed tightly. • Dysfunctional tendencies (team and individual) can limit effectiveness if not addressed and managed well. This can be in the meeting room (e.g. ineffective team dynamics) or lack of self-regulation in individual behaviour.

Table 3: Communication platforms

Description	Pros	Cons
Social media Twitter, Facebook, Yammer, Instagram etc.	Immediate, fast paced, accessible information. Useful for updating on issues requiring immediacy. Allows real-time conversation to be had without physical proximity required.	Anonymity can encourage unconstructive behaviour and communication.
Posters/announcements Using hard copy pictorial or written materials to share information, usually used as part of a broader program.	• Useful to reinforce messages and advertise strategies, prompts and reminders. • Useful for workplaces where there are shifts of workers or employees may not have easy access to electronic communications.	Limited opportunity for feedback, questioning and enhancing understanding.

10

THE ENERGISE PHASE

Skills needed
At an individual level, the skill is being able to oscillate personal energy to set the pace for the organisation.
At a leadership and organisational level, the skill is execution.

Key question
Who is doing what by when, and how?

Key outcome
Performance.

Susan was sitting in her office drinking coffee, reflecting on the various town hall meetings she had held at over the previous two weeks. She had visited each major office in the country and rolled out the new strategic direction, detailing what it meant for each function in the business. By and large she was pleased with the way it was received. 'I'm glad we spent time together co-creating the strategy and practising how to articulate it to the wider organisation,' she thought.

Somewhere in the back of her mind she remembered the strategy professor she encountered during her MBA program who said, 'Strategy not executed is merely a good idea.' She had been reading an online article that morning in which the writer had talked about how strategy written on a page does not compare with strategy that is reflected in your weekly calendar. The author was suggesting the execution of strategy happens on a daily, weekly or monthly basis and most leaders need to actively manage their time to ensure the organisation is energised behind it and it is actually executed.

During Susan's call with her boss, José, the previous night they had discussed how she and the team had made a lot of headway in developing and articulating the strategy. She was confident the strategy they had co-developed and communicated was aligned to the mandate José had given her prior to her arrival. 'I'm confident we have set the right direction,' she told José. 'Now I've just got to make sure everyone is actually behind it ...'

There are many aspects to making sure a strategic plan actually happens. Due to the complexity involved in setting direction it is a wonder a strategy ever gets executed.

The entwined challenges of deliberating and setting the right strategy, having the right people lead the communication, having it communicated in a way that actually makes sense to everybody else, understanding the organisation levers needing to be pulled, and to adequately resource (financially, time and capability-wise) are individually complex. Then throw human beings into the mix — with their varied behaviours, attitudes, mindsets, perspectives and biases. All of these complexities lie inside the organisation. Those from the external competitive landscape and a broader business environment also serve to further complicate strategic execution.

Detailed in this chapter are a number of strategies and activities that new expat leaders will find helpful in energising themselves, the leadership team and the organisation to deliver on the promise.

Organisational equity

For a new expat leader coming to Australia, assessing the organisational culture and striving to understand the nuances sitting within the organisation is a critical first step in helping energise the organisation to move towards a revamped direction, or in some cases a whole new direction.

It is often easier to describe what is lacking than to fully articulate what is present. As every human being has their own perspectives and biases, we naturally notice what is missing relative to what we know. This does not mean we are necessarily overlooking strengths but rather we are noticing what we don't see. Described in Table 4 are eight classic cultural or behavioural issues expat leaders notice.

Having recognised what is absent is an important diagnostic step — it is helpful to recognise what it is that is not wanted. The next logical step is to then chart what it is that is wanted.

Developing a set of core values and behaviours is one of the most important outputs for a leadership team. When done well and with clarity and simplicity, they serve as a definitive guide to how every major

Table 4: Cultural and behavioural issues

Lack of:	How this appears
Urgency	Working hours appear to be between 9 a.m. to 5 p.m. only. There's a rush to the door at 5 o'clock and lunches appear to take longer and longer. Deadlines are missed regularly and external needs are often ignored or forgotten. Complacency can set in, especially if historically the organisation has been successful. A lack of urgency often shows up in organisations with a dominating market share, those operating in duopolies or monopolies, those that are government or bureaucratic in nature or those with 'cash cow products'.
Focus	Commercial leaders cannot articulate organisational priorities. Everyone seems to have different priorities and often these are competing. In some cases there are too many priorities and all seem important. Internal competitive behaviours increase as resources are spread thin and the fight for resources or visibility dilutes collaboration. Fire fighting reigns and the ability to plan and execute long-term solutions seems to be missing. At the leadership team level, no one is really sure who is in charge.
Discipline	Performance can vary at different levels and underperformance is tolerated or, in some cases, celebrated. Top performers are frustrated at their colleagues' lack of performance and often leave the organisation. Deadlines are regularly missed as speed to market is an aspiration as opposed to a reality. Blaming and excuse-making are prevalent.
Accountability	This follows from a lack of discipline. Blaming and excuse-making, not understanding who is ultimately responsible, confusion as to who owns the end decision all lead to a lack of accountability. Sometimes this is due to lack of clarity but invariably results in poor performance.
Innovation	The organisation becomes internally focused and does not look to the market to see what is happening. 'The way things have always been done around here' becomes the only way things are done. Innovation is deemed to be very important but no one has the courage to take risks or try new ideas. Collaborating with other stakeholders is frowned upon as we may 'lose our IP'. People who are innovative get frustrated as their ideas are continually blocked, often at the leadership team level. Funding for innovation is talked about but never materialises.
Collective view	The organisation promotes individuality particularly in creative endeavours. Bringing 'all of you' to work is encouraged. Conversations on how people feel are given priority. The organisational collective view is seen as secondary to the individual. Whilst this view can lead to many creative endeavours it can also lead to a lack of focus and discipline.

Lack of:	How this appears
Teamwork	Collaboration across functions or within functions is not encouraged and as a consequence people become competitive. Seeking a win–win and making efforts to relate to each other are underdeveloped. The leader with the loudest voice ends up getting the biggest prize. Fiefdoms are created and individuals are rewarded for their individual efforts, even if this flies in the face of the organisational need.

decision will be taken. With these as a framework the organisational culture is actively shaped in a way to deliver the organisational strategy.

While most organisations go through this exercise at some point, unfortunately they often end up with a generic version of their core values which reads exactly like those of their competitors. There is no differentiating value. As a result, they are of little value. However, developing a guide based on core values and behaviours can be simple, effective and sustainable as seen in the following eight-step process.

Step 1: Purpose

It starts with the leadership team answering a core question: 'What is our purpose other than making money?' This should have been addressed in the Decide Phase (see Chapter 9).

Step 2: Talking the walk

'Talking the walk' is a leadership meeting designed for the members to discuss three sets of values and actively decide on those with which to lead the organisation. For this to be successful there is an underlying assumption the team has already worked on becoming an effective team and has built up levels of trust and interpersonal skills. There are three sets of values to discuss: core, aspirational and incidental.

The **core values** are those the organisation, leaders and employees actively follow. These are the values that shape the culture, influence major decisions and, if actively followed, will be a market differentiator. In high-performing organisations there will be three to five core values and they are executed 90 per cent of the time. The core values are those defended by the leadership at every opportunity. They are the building blocks of all performance appraisals. These are the ones that, if unsaid but actively followed, would still be recognised by outsiders. Core values for well-known companies are execution for GE, design for Apple and customer service for Southwest Airlines.

Aspirational values are not quite in place yet but the leadership team wants them to be, or they are being demanded from forces inside and outside the organisation. Examples of external forces include disruptive innovation to the industry, merger or competitive product launches. Internal events might include new R&D in the pipeline, future product launches, loss of market share or new senior leadership demanding change. In many senses, aspirational values are as important as core values if the leadership team is actively trying to change the culture.

Incidental values are those that have changed through default such as a leadership vacuum, accident or history. Examples include promotion by tenure, country club behaviours, entitlement beliefs, over celebrations, no celebrations, rites of passage, over- or under-servicing of customers. The leadership team needs to examine incidental values and establish whether they will serve the organisation going forward. One quick way to check is to see if there is a conflict between the core and aspirational values and the incidental values; for teams seeking high performance there usually is and the leadership team needs to make decisions on priorities.

The output of this session is to distill the options and decide on the most important values the organisation needs to be led by. At this stage this may be just a list of key words or phrases.

Step 3: Checking the shadow

Leadership teams cast long shadows in organisations, meaning employees watch and take their cues from the behaviours of their leaders. 'Do what I do, not what I say' is a well understood, if not articulated, practice.

Once the values are agreed the leadership team needs to step back and objectively assess 'How well do we, as a group, embody these core and aspirational values?' Espousing, for example, a core value of innovation but having the leadership team display a conservative approach means the employees will always look at the leaders with cynicism, distrust and possibly dismay. If the aspirational values are exactly that, aspirational, then be open and transparent about the positioning of these aspirational values and build an understanding of why they are so important.

In my experience the most effective way to assess the leadership team shadow is to conduct a culture survey of the leadership team (only). This can be done using a range of tools. My preference is for The Leadership Circle's Culture Survey™. All team members are asked to fill in an online survey and answer questions on the ideal way they would like to see this team operating and the current reality of how this team operates.

Step 4: Putting flesh on the bones

A key mistake made by leadership teams is failing to get input and engagement from the organisation in the development of values. Teams often go away to 'do the values exercise' in isolation and return with a completed set, ready to be cascaded. The lack of buy-in increases as the values are rolled out as they are seen as being imposed and there is no understanding or appreciation of the context of their creation.

For small to medium organisations, the leadership team is better served by running exercises called 'putting flesh on the bones'. This is an active stakeholder involvement exercise where the leadership team announces the desired core values. It invites the stakeholders, most often employees but not exclusively, to put language and meaning to these key words. This develops something unique to the organisation and is relevant to the people who will live them every day.

Examples of an output of this activity is the core value of 'Work hard' which is demonstrated as 'Be proud of everything we do, every day'; collaboration may transform into 'Together, not alone' and 'One company' may be 'Building our tribe'. This process develops the narrative, giving the values life.

Once the narrative is created, next comes the work of describing the desired and undesirable behaviours. Critical here is gaining clarity on the undesirable behaviours and agreeing the actions to be taken when they are encountered. Being clear about this to the organisation establishes expectations and enables the bystanders (usually colleagues and peers) to react to undesirable behaviour so the organisation becomes self-regulating in ways to support the values.

Step 5: Navigating with symbols and stories

For an organisation to embrace a new direction of values and behaviours, it is often very helpful to use a range of symbols that are identified with the espoused values. This is known as 'making the intangible tangible'. Using symbols supports the narrative. Organisations that embrace this idea use these symbols in all documentation referring to values, behaviours and strategic direction (i.e. at every launch and at all company-wide discussions these are used to embed and reinforce the values and behaviours).

Some organisations employ professional creative agencies to create these images and symbols. Others run internal competitions for staff to create the new symbols or outsource it on freelance websites such as elance.com. Whatever model suits the organisation is fine as long as quality images are created that align with the narrative.

The leadership team can benefit from spending time in developing stories that illustrate the values in action. Such stories can come from their personal backgrounds, what the values mean to them or examples of staff who personify the desired values. The main thing is to tell stories — people remember them.

Kevin Best, an expert in how to use videos in organisations to spread desired narrative, observes that YouTube is the fastest growing search engine in the western world. Given the cost-effective nature of video and smart phone technologies, every organisation can use this channel to 'put flesh on the bones' of the desired culture by using stories to spread the word.

Step 6: Setting the ships alight

Hernán Cortés de Monroy y Pizarro led an expedition causing the fall of the Aztec Empire, bringing a large portion of mainland Mexico under the rule of the King of Castille in the early 16th century. He is famous for giving his people no choice but to attack the Aztecs and win the battle. How so? Cortés scuttled ten of his eleven ships and sent the other back to Cuba with some of the treasure. He did this so his men would have no thought (or means) of returning to Cuba. As Sun Tzu said in *The Art of War*, 'At the critical moment, the leader ... acts like one who has climbed the ladder and then kicks away the ladder behind him.'[1] There is no turning back.

A great way to do this is to officially launch the new direction in a custom-designed event (or events) with all employees involved. Whether it be on an island, in the desert, in the bush around a campfire or any other of the multitude of locations on offer, the leadership team needs to carefully plan a launch that ensures everyone understands this is special and we are not going back to the old way.

Step 7: Systemising passion

All of this is useless unless it is embedded. All the organisational systems need to be aligned including recruitment policies, employment documentation, performance management, decision making and promotion criteria. Whatever training needs to be implemented to ensure everyone understands the changes should be quickly carried out.

In the first year following the launch, quarterly reviews with every staff member should be conducted. A simple process is for the leader to discuss with each person what values they have been enjoying and embracing. Secondly, ask what values they are struggling with and what help they might need. This quickly reinforces the organisation is moving forward, never back, but is happy to help those on the journey. Over time, quarterly reviews become six-monthly and then annual reviews. Some organisations get stakeholders other than employees involved in these discussions.

The embedding process can include visual celebrations such as awards that embody the espoused values, or knowledge-sharing sessions that have a specific name and are linked to a core value.

One client with a declared value of 'Be proud of what we do, every day' started knowledge-sharing forums called 'Punching above our weight' sessions, as their international colleagues referred to the Australians as always trying to punch above their weight!

Step 8: Developing individual leaders

One of the key roles for the leader is to coach and develop their direct reports, who are members of the leadership team.

Some people often confuse weaknesses and development areas, and while they overlap they are not the same. For example, someone might have no weaknesses for their current level but have development areas for their next position. Likewise the leadership team may have development needs and therefore that same person has development needs without having weaknesses, per se. The website includes a useful process to guide the development of each leadership team member.

Conducting a review of the new expat leader

In the earlier phases we recommended an assimilation exercise be conducted to help both you and your direct reports understand each other and to accelerate agreement and understanding on how you can work well together. Taking this full circle, conducting a leader review allows you to get feedback from direct reports, in a constructive and safe manner, and to understand how you are progressing.

There's no best date, but most leaders find it helpful to conduct this meeting somewhere between weeks 16 to 20. This gives the team enough experience of working with their new leader to be able to have informed views.

A third party, someone who does not report to you, is best to facilitate the feedback session. This is often best done by the head of organisational development or someone with strong facilitation experience. The objectivity of an independent facilitator means if feedback is too personal they can diffuse it or reframe it in a business context. The facilitator needs to interview everybody individually prior to bringing the leadership team together. In the team meeting, the facilitator presents the overall information in broad themes back to you and the leadership group at the same time. This allows everyone to hear all the feedback simultaneously, for you to ask questions to seek clarity or understanding, and for the group to go deep with the feedback, if required.

There are five areas of enquiry and feedback to cover in such a meeting, as outlined in Table 5.

Table 5: Areas of feedback

Topic area	Typical response areas
What have you positively noticed about [name] since they arrived as our new leader?	• Communication skills. • Relationship skills. • Business knowledge. • Past experience. • Discipline. • Passion/enthusiasm. • Ability to learn the local context. • Ability to listen.
What have you noticed about [name] since they arrived that might be getting in their way?	• Their viewpoint. • Perspectives and biases. • Urgency to act without information. • Influence on group dynamics. • Lack of listening skills.
What would you like [name] to do over the next twelve months?	• Set a clear direction. • Continue to lead. • Continue to listen. • Seek broader input to decisions. • Understand the marketplace more thoroughly. • Change certain behaviours that are getting in the way. • Be more visible to the organisation. • Change their personal style.
What does [name] need to know to be successful in the next twelve months?	• The company culture. • A history of the organisation. • The context in which decisions have traditionally been made. • The broader marketplace. • Our products and services in depth. • Why Australia is different to other countries. • Leadership styles in Australia.
What can we the leadership team do to support [name] in the leadership role?	• Understand their intention in more detail. • Get behind the new strategy and direction. • Actively work to develop the organisational culture. • Speak with the same voice. • Cascade communications down the organisation in unison. • Be seen to support the new leader in public meetings.

11

THE REVIEW AND RENEW PHASE

Skills needed

At an individual level, the skill is in energy oscillation to maintain your performance energy and focus to play a long game.

At a leadership team level, the skill is adaptability in continually reviewing progress, reshaping focus and renewing execution efforts through a series of programs.

Key question

How do we build in sustainable processes to ensure the organisation ends up where we are guiding it?

Key outcome

Sustained change through programs.

'I'm tired,' said Susan. 'This has been one hell of a ride.' Susan's coach had asked her how she was feeling after eight months in the role. He smiled at her response. 'That's what most people say at this stage,' he said, 'and yet the hard work is still ahead! You've done a great job in setting the scene for change and driving the organisation toward that. Now it's important you monitor yourself so you can continually review and, where needed, recalibrate and renew your focus and energy levels. The focus now needs to be on sustainability, yours and the organisation's.'

Susan was glad she was using an external coach who specialised in transitions. She was not sure if she would have been able to manage the continual and varied challenges and changes without having someone impartial as a soundboard. Even though she knew she was doing a good job and indeed José, her boss, had commented so, sometimes Susan felt quite alone. She valued the trust and advice her coach was sharing. 'Let's talk about sustainability,' she said.

'There are two levels of sustainability that we need to discuss,' her coach said. 'Sustainability in the organisation, which often refers to accountability, and sustainability at the individual level. Let's start there ...'

Sustaining the individual

Given the reality of ever-present change in societies and organisations, it is surprising how poor organisations are in training executives to manage transitions well. Also, given the failure rates of expat transitions, one would assume organisations would spend more time ensuring their executives are competent at both transitions and execution.

While the development of executive education programs has expanded the collective understanding of theories across a wide domain of knowledge, the flattening of organisational hierarchies means there is less mentoring, informal or otherwise, happening across executive ranks. The tacit knowledge that sits within the executive ranks is often untapped and therefore newer executives are not benefiting from the experiences of their peers. The practical know-hows and the translation of theory into reality is often allowed to walk out the door when executives leave.

Yet all the research studies that refer to talent development at senior levels underline the importance of having experience and expertise in transition management. We know the high rate of failures in mergers, acquisitions, integrations as well as executive transitions. Ultimately, these failures boil down to failing to execute on the desired outputs and take people through the transition. Leaders have become skilled at understanding the need for change, developing strategies and communicating them in different platforms. However, the real skill of embedding change as continual renewal processes remains poorly executed.

Around week 20 you will need to invest in reviewing and, if needed, reshaping your leadership so as to create a viable and sustainable approach. This can continue to the end of your first year and beyond. The following detail some ideas and areas of focus that can support this stage.

Feeling tired in the eighth month, as Susan mentioned to her coach, is a very common phenomenon and, if not managed well, can lead to burnout. Going through any transition can be taxing and can include (but is not limited to) physical, emotional and mental stresses. This is the experience of many expatriates as they navigate the multiple layers of transitions and challenges. These personal stresses need to be managed in the context of the ongoing pressure to continue at high levels of work performance while meeting the expectations of not only themselves but also the important people around them including family, their team and the organisation. If not managed well this compounds the pressure and increases the downward spiral to underperformance and breakdown.

The concept of maintaining a peak performance state in the face of sustained pressure has its origins in the sporting world. The strategies translate well into the commercial arena and are a useful resource for executives who find themselves in this predicament. The following strategies provide and maintain the energy for executives to continue to strive forward, often in challenging and difficult circumstances. The strategies can be classified as the '5Rs' — resolve, readiness, reflection, resilience and rest.

Resolve

This is about clarity of aspiration. It is being clear about what 'good' *looks and feels like* and passionately believing it is attainable. Your resolve provides the fuel to maintain the drive and focus towards goal attainment.

Key to developing resolve is being able to describe and connect with the feelings you want to experience — intellectually, physically and emotionally. A recent client described what it would feel like when leading at his best: 'It feels like I am driving a racing car — heightened senses, on full alert, aware of all changes in environment, masterfully in control of the vehicle, sensing and responding, centred and confident and I am certainly having fun.'

There is a strong positive relationship between self-efficacy and work performance. Self-efficacy enhances and supports mental and physical health and influences self-regulation to enable setting loftier goals; be more able to resist disruptions, persevere and problem-solve as a result of being task-focused. This means creating and holding a clear experience about how you, as an expat leader, want to feel in the performance of your role. It can also be translated to a broader view of how you want to feel about your entire expatriate experience and also what you wish for the experience of your family.

Resolve is critical as it motivates persistence. It is more enjoyable and fruitful than goals but actually provides the basis for creating meaningful goals. Central to this notion is the acknowledgement and acceptance that resolve cannot exist without freedom and responsibility. The leader has an internal locus of control in that they acknowledge they have choice and the freedom to act and are responsible for their own actions.

Readiness

This is the group of physical, mental and emotional strategies and activities employed to attain the desired state and, as such, create the desired feelings on an ongoing basis. When done in alignment it is an enjoyable process, not a chore, as 'doing the preparation' is an integral part of the performance and the pathway to achievement.

Alignment is achieved when the preparation is connected through the development of useful goals. This maintains desire and energy while giving the skills to excel. When working with clients we at OSullivanField suggest to them that goals can be both outcome- and learning-based. In fact, as an expat leader, your goals need to be both outcome- and learning-orientated as the achievement of outcomes and learning new skills will guarantee your success. Their achievement may depend on you learning and executing new skills or expanding your repertoire to do some things differently.

This covers the concerted groundwork required to ensure there is the competence to execute at the standard needed for successful performance. For example, an outcome goal might be to drive a particular commercial objective. A learning goal might be to develop stage presence when peaking at organisational town halls. In his book *The Tipping Point*, Malcolm Gladwell says it takes 10,000 hours of practice to achieve mastery.[1] As I have outlined throughout this book, there are many skills to develop as an expat leader and one cannot assume mastery in all of them.

The second part to readiness is the importance of staying or becoming physically fit. Most executives underestimate the cognitive increase they undertake when promoted to a new role. Mental alertness is positively and negatively affected by one's level of physical fitness. As with many groups in society, executives are relatively healthy and fit while in their teenage years and early twenties. This slows down as we get older and start having children. Then we reach our forties and fifties and fitness is often long forgotten. Yet, ironically, this is when we are at our most senior in organisations and being physically fit is an imperative to assist us in the performance of being an executive.

I occasionally remind clients of the famous DeLorean sports car in the *Back to the Future* movies starring Michael J. Fox in the 1980s. John DeLorean, who created the infamous car, said at the time it was a sports car designed for twenty-year-olds but only 50-year-olds could afford it. Likewise a body that was designed for the twenty-year-old is the one the 50-year-old actually needs to perform their executive role well!

Resilience

A definition of resilience is the property of a material that enables it to resume its original shape or position after being bent, stretched or compressed: elasticity. Ironically, sometimes this is how we as individuals can feel — out of shape, stretched to our limit or compressed to our former selves after being through stressful experiences or when we are not feeling very resilient.

Sustaining high levels of performance cannot be achieved without experiencing and overcoming obstacles. The obstacles may be internal, such as anxiety or self-doubt, or external, such as resistance or dissatisfaction in the team, organisation or family. These obstacles are to be expected, and, as such, when they are encountered the strategy is to embrace rather than resist or retreat from them. You need the ability to bounce back when those challenging and difficult times come up and things don't go as planned. It's really the capacity to be able to deal with the disappointment, fear or other responses that emerge when times are tough.

When obstacles are encountered, the process for the expat is to first reconnect with the feelings associated with resolve. The reconnection to this state helps to gain clarity and perspective about its meaning. This fuels the motivation to continue working hard, to develop and execute new strategies and skills to overcome the obstacles.

There are numerous practices that can be utilised to develop resilience, many of which are rooted in the emerging field of positive psychology. Some popular ones include being solution focused in seeking what can be done and taking accountability and responsibility for action; developing and maintaining relationships; showing appreciation and gratitude; taking a big-picture perspective and relating the ideas we have discussed here; being clear on goals and continuing learning. These peak performance strategies, when identified, practised and implemented, are very powerful resources and tools to use in your attempts to achieve success.

Reflection

The reflective period occurs after encountering an obstacle. This is about creating *a shaft of stillness* where you can think, process and understand what is happening. Reflection is an important step as it suspends the urge to follow blind pathways and prevents the expatriate being caught in the obstacle–preparation loop which is grinding away without progress.

Revisiting your reasons for undertaking this assignment can rekindle your motivation. It reenergises and, as a result, new or modified goals might emerge to allow engagement with meaningful preparation. In working with your coach you can examine what has happened and define the learnings so as to develop a constructive forward path.

Rest

They say the greatest enemy of sustained peak performance is lack of rest. It is unrealistic and unsustainable to continually operate at full throttle.

The product of working like this is 'burnout' or breakdown. Peak performance requires oscillation in energy and effort, with adequate rest and rejuvenation so that the resources are available to perform when required.

When there are pressures for performance and you are 'new' to an organisation, there can be a tendency to work extended hours without adequate physical and mental rest. It is critically important that both physical and mental rest are scheduled into your plan to ensure there is the 'fuel' to continue to drive the performance in a sustained manner.

When Joe arrived in Sydney from New Zealand he had previously had a successful career in practice management. Leading a turnaround of the Australian business, nine months later he found himself exhausted, always busy, readily distracted and having conversations with his wife where she suggested she was quite unhappy with the way he was working.

What many executives fail to remember is that time is finite. Most resources and organisations are not, but time is. Joe had to actively sit down and work out a calendar that allowed him to plan his days, weeks and months so he was face-to-face with people when they needed it most yet he had enough time by himself to think and plan for the business. This meant coming to the office at 7 a.m. and having two hours uninterrupted to focus on overseas emails and any urgent events that had happened overnight. It meant during the day between 11 a.m. and 3 p.m. he was available to be around the business with staff, in meetings or with customers. He changed his diary to make sure he had a minimal amount of late-night meetings and kept every Tuesday and Thursday free so he could concentrate on his family rather than overseas business calls. Building in a fitness schedule four times a week allowed him to lose the kilos he had put on over the previous two years and to regain the energy he had lost.

Within three months Joe was remarking to friends he was sleeping better than he had ever done before and seemed to be thinking more clearly at work.

This is not an isolated story. One of the main causes for lack of success in leadership transitions is the lack of self-management in the second half of the first year. There are cycles executives fall into that, if not managed, can lead to exhaustion, lack of direction and poor execution of the original plans.

One area of pre-emption that we lead our clients through is to look out for signs and symptoms of potential burnout. These include the following:

Not staying focused

Creative leaders often have many ideas and if they have poor self-management can vocalise these new ideas in conversations with colleagues and staff. Due to their position, the ideas are often misunderstood to be directives or strategies rather than purely an idea being shared. Other leaders who are unsure of the strategy or who are not confident in backing themselves in the strategy often fall into the trap of trying many different things. Both leaders come across as unfocused, unclear and reactive. The organisation ends up being very, very busy without getting the important things done.

Not occasionally closing the door

Having an open-door policy became the vogue in the 1990s. It suggested the leader was happy to have conversations and was open to people dropping by. The downside, however, is that the leader has no time alone to think. Ultimately, the more senior a leader the more they get paid to think on behalf of the organisation. Not blocking time off to prepare for meetings, to analyse data ahead of decision making and to think about the future, means the leader ends up being reactive. In a desire to integrate into the culture, many expat leaders end up spending no time alone, which creates what they are trying to avoid — diluted leadership capability.

Not being aware of one's ability

Socrates was right when he said 'Know thyself'. Knowing your strengths and weaknesses means being able to plan to accommodate weaknesses and to complement them with people who have strengths in your gaps. The leadership assessment in Chapter 6 can serve as a guide to where gaps may be. However, other areas will emerge in the first six months after your arrival. For example, for natives of non-English speaking countries, thinking in their primary language yet speaking in English means their presentation skills can be affected. They often give the impression of rambling or taking too long to come to the point. This is a potential gap of which they would have been unaware pre-arrival. Not seeking out feedback on where they can improve, particularly from trusted colleagues, means the gap will always remain.

Not being aware of inherent bias

As described earlier, everybody has natural perspectives, mindsets and biases they have built up over their career and lifetime. Leaders who have developed a career through commercial paths, particularly sales, generally have a natural bias for action. Leaders who come up through the finance routes, particularly via an audit team, have a natural bias towards analysis. Leaders who have emerged through marketing, particularly creative marketing, have a natural bias towards 'blue sky' thinking.

Understanding your biases ensures you do not filter and discount information that may go against your natural bias; it will ensure you don't fall into the trap of self-illusion. As the stakes get higher in organisations, people's tendency to be vulnerable and open to their biases diminishes, often leading to mistakes.

Not making the tough decisions

As discussed earlier, an Australian research study found most leaders regretted not taking action sooner when it came to poor performance by one of their direct reports. The desire to fit into a new role and country can often lead to over-accommodating people's complacencies or avoiding tough issues. Remember: the role of a leader is to lead and this means making decisions. The irony is that many decisions lead to more work to be done. However this is not necessarily a bad thing.

Not displaying good judgement

One of the great privileges of expatriate leaders is working with executives who are on the fast-track for promotion. While these people are undoubtedly talented, it is not uncommon for them to demonstrate poor judgement, whether in isolated incidents or as a pattern of behaviour. The upshot is it derails their career. Exhibition of judgement, whether good or bad, is a moderator of executive potential. Bad habits, developed early, can come back to haunt the expatriate when they are on a much bigger stage and under a bigger spotlight. Behaviours and reactions that have limited impact when a frontline, junior or even mid-level manager can be somewhat quarantined. When the effect of the poor judgement is expanded due to the impacts of the executive being at functional, country or regional level, this can have a parallel negative impact on the assessment of the executive's capability and performance to the point where it caps their advancement.

Sustaining the organisation

If not done already, there are four important if not obvious organisational structural processes to implement that will go towards sustaining the organisation en route towards a desired destination of performance.

The *cycle of cascading key objectives* from the strategic level to individual level in every function is important. Albeit very obvious, this is regularly overlooked within organisations. When employees cannot see how their role and its outputs relate to where the organisation is headed, their motivation and discretionary effort drops. Researchers Teresa Amabile and Steven Kramer suggest that motivation is regulated most by when employees receive feedback on their performance *as it relates* to the organisation's outputs and goals.[2]

Quarterly business reviews and updates are both a communication process and a business ownership process. The involvement of key employees one and two layers below the leadership team in the regular review of the organisation increases a sense of ownership in the organisation's progress. Publicly sharing the progress in an open town hall meeting with all staff ensures everyone is involved.

Ensure everyone has a clear line of sight towards how they can improve the organisation, then create a *bonus or reward system* that recognises and rewards them for doing so. One client originally from the United Kingdom and in the interior design and flooring industry, came to Australia to manage the Australian and New Zealand affiliates. He was pleasantly surprised at the increase in levels of ownership and proactivity the employees demonstrated once they understood the company's objectives and were rewarded on improvements towards the same.

Lastly, undertaking a *360-degree process of the leadership team members and their impact on the overall organisation* is a great way to ensure alignment and recognition by the wider organisation that the team is serious about leading the organisation as espoused. There are many tools available to do this and some organisations use internally developed models. When asked to facilitate this process I recommend The Leadership Circle Profile™ 360-degree tool as it works really well alongside The Leadership Circle Culture Survey™ previously mentioned. The tool is very well researched regarding the factors that foster leadership progress such as Relating, Self-awareness, Integrity, Systems Thinking and Achieving while also measuring factors that may reduce leadership effectiveness, including Compliance, Protecting and Aggression.

PART 3

SUPPORT

12

THE JOURNEY CONTINUES

Two years after she'd begun her expat assignment, Susan stood up for the final time to address the Town Hall. She remembered her first day walking into the building feeling both cocksure and nervous. As she looked around the room she realised how many relationships had been built in the previous two years. She also realised how much of an impact they'd had on her. As she thanked the organisation for welcoming her to Australia she reminded them of how far the organisation had come over the last number of years. She talked about her pride in being part of that journey and all the things she had learnt along the way. Her natural sense of humour was displayed as she recounted several mistakes made along the way and memorable episodes she had experienced.

Susan was proud that Scottie, the local commercial head, was now being promoted to managing director to succeed her. As he gave her a hug on the stage the organisation cheered and wished Susan well in her next role as Regional Head in Latin America. She left Australia the following week with a family who had shared an adventure and as her husband, Joe, said as they boarded the plane, 'Sydney, you won over our hearts'.

Over dinner with her coach before she left, Susan shared her most memorable moments of their relationship and where the steep learning curves along the way had emerged. She also shared with him the leadership practices she had built up while in Australia that she now intended to take into her new role. 'You know, I realised the other day when I was saying goodbye to the organisation,' she said to her coach, 'this leadership journey never finishes, does it?' 'Never,' he said, 'and that's a good thing.'

The journey of an expat leader usually leads to another expat role before either settling at a particular level of organisational leadership or getting promoted to global levels of leadership. The ongoing business changes and issues never stop coming. People will always surprise you! The need to develop oneself as a leader never stops.

In my role at Sydney Business School, where I lecture on the Masters Degree in Business Coaching, I get to work with great students. They are typically senior level executives in their mid-forties who are choosing to study out of interest and passion. At some stage in the semester I get them to do an exercise called 'Insights from the future version of yourself'. Essentially this is where the 90-year-old self writes a letter to the current self. The exercise is in two parts. In the first part the 90-year-old offers insight into the next 40 or 50 years. Given the individuality of each person, the insights vary enormously.

The second part of the exercise is a set question, which is: If you stay doing the work that you do, why would you?[1] Interestingly, the answers every year are consistent across the groups of students. Most commonly they are:

- I love what I do because it is meaningful work and adds value to others.
- I get to work with great people who inspire me to do great work.
- I am empowered to do what I need to do and want to do. I lead in a way that empowers others to do what they need to do.

When I ask the groups what might get in the way of achieving those desired outcomes (I know they are very strongly desired as the emotion involved when sharing the answers is so palpable!) the answer is always the same. The one major potential block to achieving those outcomes is the person themselves (i.e. they won't continue to develop to the level needed to achieve the desired outcomes they seek).

The journey always continues.

RESOURCES

I hope you have found this book useful on your expat leadership journey down under to Australia. Following are a series of websites that may be useful. Handouts and worksheets referred to in the book are available online, ready for printout at www.foreignerincharge.com.

General expat information

American Citizens Abroad (ACA)
www.aca.ch

British Expats
www.britishexpats.com

Expatriate news, information and community
www.expatica.com

Expat Focus
www.expatfocus.com

Expat Focus: city guides
http://expatfocus.com/cities

Expat Focus: country guides
http://expatfocus.com/countries

Expat Exchange
www.expatexchange.com

Expat Expert
www.expatexpert.com

The Foreign Wives Club
www.foreignwivesclub.com

World Health Organization
The WHO website contains detailed health information for countries worldwide.
www.who.int

Websites about Australia

Australian Government Travel Advisory and Consular Assistance Service
www.smartraveller.gov.au

Visa information
www.immi.gov.au/Services/Pages/online-services.aspx

Australian Capital Territory (ACT) and Canberra
www.act.gov.au
www.visitcanberra.com.au

Queensland and Brisbane
www.qld.gov.au
www.visitbrisbane.com.au

New South Wales and Sydney
www.nsw.gov.au
www.cityofsydney.nsw.gov.au

Northern Territory
www.nt.gov.au
www.tourismtopend.com.au

South Australia
www.sa.gov.au
www.southaustralia.com

Tasmania
www.tas.gov.au
www.discovertasmania.com.au

Victoria and Melbourne
www.vic.gov.au
www.thatsmelbourne.com.au

Western Australia and Perth
www.wa.gov.au
http://visitperthcity.com

Schools

Education system
www.immi.gov.au

Catholic education system
www.ncec.catholic.edu.au

Anglican school system
www.anglicanschoolsaustralia.ed.au

Selective schools
http://bettereducation.com.au/SelectiveSchoolView0.aspx
http://house.ksou.cn/topschool.php?filter=selective&sta=nsw
http://det.wa.edu.au/curriculumsupport/giftedandtalented/detcms/navigation/parents/selective-schools/

Private schools
www.privateschoolsdirectory.com.au
www.privateschoolsguide.com

Main sports
AFL (Aussie rules)
www.afl.com.au

Cricket
www.cricket.com.au

Netball
http://netball.com.au

Rugby league
www.nrl.com

Rugby union
www.rugby.com.au

Soccer
www.footballaustralia.com.au

ENDNOTES

Introduction

1. Towers Watson 2012, Worldwide ERC 2012 Global Talent Mobility Study, accessed at www.towerswatson.com/en/Press/2012/07/Despite-Cost-Pressures-Multinationals-Plan-to-Increase-International-Assignments-in-Next-Two-Years.
2. Lee Hecht Harrison, 2012, 'No onboarding practices? A "sink or swim" approach is risky business', 'Insights' report.
3. World Development Bank, Expatriate Report, 2010.

Chapter 1

1. *Forbes* magazine 2013.
2. Personal communication via third party.
3. Black, J.S., Morrison, A.J. and Gregersen, H.B., 1999, *Global Explorers: The next generation of leaders,* Routledge, Milton Park, p. 20.
4. 'The Expatriate Experience in Australia', CEO Forum Group, November 2012.

Chapter 3

1. Bryson, D.R. and Hoge, C.M., 2005, *A Portable Identity: A woman's guide to maintaining a sense of self while moving overseas,* Transition Press International, Maryland.

Chapter 5

1. Watkins, M., 2003, *The First 90 Days: Critical success strategies for new leaders at all levels,* Harvard Business Review Press, Boston.
2. Bradt, G., Check, J. and Pedraza, J. 2009, *The New Leader's 100-Day Action Plan: How to take charge, build your team, and get immediate results,* John Wiley & Sons, Inc, Hoboken.

3. Adapted from Charan, R., Drotter, S. and Noel, J., 2000, *The Leadership Pipeline: How to build the leadership powered company*, Jossey-Bass, San Francisco.

Chapter 6

1. Harris, P., Moran, T. and Moran, S., 2004, *Managing Cultural Differences: Global leadership strategies for the 21st century*, Elsevier Butterworth-Heinemann, Oxford.
2. Tucker, M.F. and Baier, V.E., 1982, 'Research background for the Overseas Assessment Inventory', paper presented to the SIETAR International Conference, San Antonio, Texas.
3. Goldsmith, M., 2007, *What Got You Here Won't Get You There: How successful people become even more successful*, Profile Books Ltd, London.

Chapter 7

1. Mackey, J. and Sisodia, R., 2013, *Conscious Capitalism: Liberating the heroic spirit of business*, Harvard Business Review Publishing, Boston.

Chapter 8

1. Watkins. M, 2003, *The First 90 Days: Critical success strategies for new leaders at all levels*, Harvard Business Review Press, Boston.
2. Grant, A.M. and Greene, J., 2001, *Coach Yourself*, Pearson Education Ltd, Harlow.
3. Church, M., Stein, S. and Henderson, M., 2011, *Thought Leaders*, Harper Collins, Auckland.
4. www.theleadershipcircle.com/wp-content/uploads/2011/05/07_SpiritOfLeadership.pdf
5. Lencioni, P., 1998, *The Five Dysfunctions of a Team: A leadership fable*, Jossey-Bass, San Francisco.
6. Gallup, 2013, *The State of the Global Workplace: Employee engagement insights for business leaders worldwide*, accessed at www.gallup.com/strategicconsulting/164735/state-global-workplace.aspx.
7. 'Managing in an era of mistrust', Maritz Poll 2010, accessed at www.maritz.com.
8. Table adapted from Watkins, M., 2003, *The First 90 Days: Critical success strategies for new leaders at all levels*, Harvard Business Review Publishing, Boston.
9. Schein, E., 1992, *Organizational Culture and Leadership*, (2nd ed.), Jossey-Bass, San Francisco.
10. www.theleadershipcircle.com/assessment-tools/survey.

Chapter 9

1. Katzenbach, J. and Smith, D., 1993, *The Wisdom of Teams: Creating the high-performance organization*, Harvard Business School Press, Boston.
2. Hawkins, P., 2011, *Leadership Team Coaching: Developing collective transformational leadership*, Kogan Page, London.
3. www.ted.com/talks/simon_sinek_how_great_leaders_inspire_action.html.
4. Zak, P.J., Stanton, A.A. and Ahmadi, S., 2007, 'Oxytocin increases generosity in humans', *PLoS ONE* 2(11): e1128. doi:10.1371/journal.pone.0001128.
5. Torres, R. and Tollman, P., 2013, 'Debunking the myths of the first 100 days', accessed at https://www.bcgperspectives.com/content/articles/leadership_human_resources_debunking_the_myths_of_the_first_100_days.
6. I was involved in an interview study of business leaders in between 1999 and 2003. Unpublished.

Chapter 10

1. Tzu, S., *The Art of War*, Translated by Thomas Cleary, Shambhala Publications Boston & London, 1988.

Chapter 11

1. Gladwell, M., 2000, *The Tipping Point: How little things can make a big difference*, Little, Brown & Company, New York.
2. Amabile, T. and Kramer, S., 2011, *The Progress Principle: Using small wins to ignite joy, engagement, and creativity at work*, Harvard Business Review Press, Boston.

Chapter 12

1. Adapted from Goldsmith, M., 2007, *What Got You Here Won't Get You There: How successful people become even more successful*, Profile Books Ltd, London.

ACKNOWLEDGEMENTS

A book like this does not write itself. If a whole village raises a child then a group of professionals and family members write a book. Many thanks to all of these people who helped birth this creation.

To my clients, who have taught me more than I will ever teach them. Their dedication to leading well across borders is inspiring. Our world is in good hands if some of the leaders I have encountered are in charge.

To colleagues across the industry, including Drs Grace McCarthy, Gordon Spence, Julia and Trenton Milner and all of our students at Sydney Business School, Praesta International and all their coaches who became great mentors and friends over the years, Robin Linnecar, who encouraged me, Peter Hawkins for being an integrationist, Tony Grant and Marshall Goldsmith for blazing the way, Will Linssen for facilitating the process, Peter Shaw for encouraging me in a Dublin hotel bar to write for my clients, Karen Gee for guiding the writing of this book, Naomi the best transcriber ever, Roma and Pauline at The Leadership Circle, Nicky, Jamie, Brian, Jed, Tony, David, Mark, Stephen, David and all of those who offered insightful comments to the evolving manuscript.

To the 'family' in our office. Thanks to you all for your support, ideas and dedication to serving our clients as best as we can and do.

To my family in Ireland. Travelling and living abroad can be a great adventure but you always leave someone behind. We miss and love you all.

To Grace, Osh, Lara, Addie and Kitty. What fabulous kids to have and to learn from. Life is never dull. Thankfully.

To Carole who supervised the writing of every chapter, threw in great ideas and removed the rubbish ones. She has always encouraged me to be the best I can be, to think bigger and to serve as many people as possible. Without her nothing would have happened. She would say that by being with her all things are possible. In a very Australian sense I am a 'lucky, lucky bastard'!

INDEX